THE TEACHINGS OF JESUS
Edited by JOHN H. KERR, D. D.

THE TEACHING OF JESUS CONCERNING GOD THE FATHER

Archibald Thomas Robertson, D. D.

THE TEACHING OF JESUS

CONCERNING

GOD THE FATHER

By

Archibald Thomas Robertson, D. D.

Wipf and Stock Publishers

EUGENE, OREGON

Wipf and Stock Publishers
199 West 8th Avenue, Suite 3
Eugene, Oregon 97401

The Teaching of Jesus Concerning God the Father
By Robertson, A.T.
ISBN: 1-57910-171-2
Publication date: October, 1998
Previously published by American Tract Society, October, 1998 .

TO MY FATHER

WHOSE LOVE IS

KIN TO THAT OF GOD THE FATHER.

CONTENTS

CHAPTER I

The Importance of a Knowledge of God. Modern Ideas about God.

"None is good save one, even God" (Mark x. 18).

THE picture of a world without God is horrible to contemplate. A world without God in fact would be either chaos or death. An orderly world is not possible apart from mind and a mind commensurate with so vast a problem. To admit that mind is to admit God. But the world can be without God even if God exists. Practically this state is nearly as bad as the other, though not quite, for even those who have "no hope" and are "without God in the world" (Eph. ii. 12) are near God if they only knew it, for "he is not far from each one of us" (Acts xvii. 27).

Hope for a Godless World

For if God exists, he can be found. Though our search for him be not successful as we grope in the dark, if haply we may feel after him and find him, still we need not despair. Some point of contact may be found between us and God that may, when discovered, open the door of heaven, as Helen Keller was led by touch to God. But atheism is essentially pessimistic and so Paul correctly said that those who have not God have no hope. The reflex influence of one's belief in God cannot be overestimated. What one thinks about God determines his theology, his philosophy, his ethical views, his conduct. The ground of hope for a world without God is that the Father seeks to manifest himself to men. This is the positive word that Christ has for men, this is the mainspring in Christian missions, this is the crown of human destiny, to be found of God.

Why the World was Without a Knowledge of God

If the evolutionary view of the world's origin be correct, it does not follow that originally men did not have adequate knowledge of God. Certainly the Scriptures teach original knowledge of God and many scientists find much to confirm it. In the most primitive and savage of present peoples some knowledge of a superior being is preserved with hints of better knowledge in other days. Names of God occur in all parts of the earth and memory of better days exists. It is true that, while Christianity is God seeking man, heathenism is man seeking God,—true in a sense only, however. Heathenism is much more a distinct departure from God than it is a groping after the unknown God on the part of a few. Certainly the fall of man after reaching the image of God is possible. We witness human degradation in lives around us. Progress in arts and sciences does not measure progress in goodness. There is a strange persistence, if not increase, of evil through the centuries where the restraint of fear of God does not abide. The facts of human nature do not justify us in saying that sin is merely the remnant of the animal nature brought on from our animal ancestry. Sin is far more of the spirit than of the flesh. It is an easy way of shirking responsibility for wrongdoing to charge it to our animal nature. Evolution as an agent fails to explain the origin of man. Evolution as God's method of working can offer an adequate explanation of man's history.

The problem of the origin of evil and so of man's alienation from God is the most difficult in theology, so difficult in fact that some who believe in God deny the existence of sin. But this again is to win serenity of spirit at the cost of the evidence of the senses. We are helpless to speak a sure word on this subject if we decline to admit the existence of Satan who threw man down from his pedestal and won men away from the worship of God. The chief end of man is to know God and to be like him. It is ruin enough to satisfy any devil if he could thwart the true destiny of men. The three ultimate realities are God, self, the world ; and a recent writer has well said that science works from the point of view of the world, philosophy from that of self, and theology from that of God. Each of these great methods has its place and value, but surely the supreme value belongs to theology if it can really gain the standpoint of God. To see man as God sees him would be theology indeed, and not philosophy under the garb of theology. As God looks upon man and man's sin, what does he see? He sees the truth and all the truth. "Can man by searching find out God?"

What the World now Thinks about God

One of the worst heretics is the man who is afraid that his views may be wrong and is afraid to investigate the facts. Cowardice before facts is pitiable. Repression of the intellect as to religious problems has its necessary reaction in scepticism. The victory for individual opinion won by Luther against the tyranny of Roman Catholic stifling of the mind was bound to lead to defiant atheism. The pendulum will swing its course. But better this than the blight of mediæval authority over the human mind, for the facts of the universe are open to all. The atheist has had his say and he speaks largely to an unsympathetic audience at present. The blatant infidel has a coterie of followers here and there among the openly wicked, but not among the real men of culture. Materialism is no longer a word with which to frighten the followers of God. Haeckel has only a small following among true scientists. Science has won its place against an intolerant theology and has also realized its helplessness to explain the universe without God. Science cannot tell what "life" is nor consciousness nor ethics. The retreat to agnosticism is no longer formidable. Even Sir Leslie Stephen cannot revive it. This essentially apologetic position has been obliged to concede a Force behind the world of matter, grudgingly admitting the failure of materialism though unwilling to affirm the personality of this Force. But the hesitation of Spencer is passing into the positive affirmation of Lord Kelvin, who openly asserts that science has a definite message in behalf of the existence of God. The best scientific and religious spirit of our time is seeking a higher unity in the realm of spirit in the common acknowledgment of God as Creator and Lord of all. The subtle pantheism of Spinoza reappears in the still popular monism. But one cannot think that this is the ultimate philosophy of man nor the true explanation of the world as it is, any more than the idealism of Hegel. Our time has passed from the cold deism of the eighteenth century with its absentee God.

The spiritual interpretation of the universe holds the field once more. The doctrine of the immanence of God is more clearly perceived in our day than ever, but needs to be reinforced by the parallel truth of the transcendence of God. In a word the modern mind is open to faith in God. Evolution, instead of ruling God out of the world, has restored him to his true place in the minds of scientific men. The return of George J. Romanes and John Fiske to belief in a personal God is symptomatic of the age. The modern world is not so patient with mediæval theological distinctions, but is deeply impressed with the idea of the Fatherhood of God. The historic Christ fills the horizon of modern scholarship and that scholarship is reacting to the admission that he is the eternal Christ, the Son of God. The counter movement of Ritschlianism is impatient with the historic realities and cares most for the ideas gathered up into Christianity. The great controversy of our time is taking shape around the Person of Christ, whether in truth he were in fact and essence the Son of God, God in nature, or merely so accepted by those who elevated him by faith to the position of deity. The outcome cannot be doubted, but meanwhile many will be led into the bog of Ritschlianism, the most subtle apologetic of all time for holding on to the form and surrendering the substance of Christianity. The Holy Spirit in his work in the present age is apprehended in a new and vital sense. Judaism itself accents still the fact of God and that much of truth even Mohammedanism proclaims. In fact God is the central fact of human thinking, and this fact was never more clearly recognized than now. The theologies of all time are two—one with God as the center, the other with man as the center. Even now with all the new interest in man the God-centered theology is dominant. Some systems still betray a certain "*horror dei*," but the modern mind as a whole uncovers itself before the idea of God.

Has God a Clear Word about Himself

It is freely granted that God cannot be defined. The saying is eminently true: "Le Dieu defini est le dieu fini." The infinite God cannot be grasped by the human mind either by inquiry or by revelation. It is impossible for God fully to manifest himself to men, but this fact does not mean that God cannot at all reveal himself to some men. Plato went as far as the unaided human intellect can go in its speculation about God, but he gave up and hoped for more light. "We will wait," said he, "for one, be it God or God-inspired man, to teach us our religious duties and to take away the darkness from our eyes." If evolution stops short of opening men's eyes to God, can revelation sufficiently remove scales from the eyes of the heart for God to be seen? Our day has an answer that steadies many hearts when it points and appeals to the consciousness of the individual Christian as a sure anchor in a time of cold criticism and harassing doubts about the Bible itself. There is force in this appeal that God shows himself to the humble heart that seeks him in trust. And yet everything must not be made to rest on the experimental argument, for the Mohammedan and the Buddhist may make a similar appeal. We still need the appeal to the life as shown in the outward expression of the inward experience. We still need the argument from design in nature, now greatly reinforced by evolution. We still need the Word of God, the Scriptures, historical and human, colored by time and circumstance, and yet speaking a new and growing and luminous and illuminating message from God himself about himself.

God reveals himself not all at once, but slowly, now one attribute, now another, the God of history and God in history. Even in Homer Zeus is called *pater* (father) and Jupiter among the Romans is the same word and idea. But God the Father was lost in an Olympus of contending gods and goddesses. If God the Father was to be known by men, there was need of a clear word of reassurance from him. The distinctive message of Christianity is just at this point. It claims that Jesus as God is able to reveal God to men as never before known. It is not enough to listen to the voice of nature that in silent grandeur points us to

God. It is not enough to hearken to the heaven-born aspirations that cry out after God nor the lofty speculations of the reason about God. Better than these is the sure word of prophecy in the Scriptures, a lamp shining in a dark place. But best of all is Jesus Christ himself who claims to bring God to men. He comes with the approval of the Father himself: "This is my beloved son, in whom I am well pleased; hear ye him" (Matthew xvii. 5). What has the Son to say about the Father? We would see Jesus for his own sake, but for more, wonderful as that is. He bears a message from the Father and is the image of the Father. In the Son then we may study the Father with reverence and fear. In this book we shall "hear" the Son on this greatest of all themes, about his Father and our Father.

CHAPTER II

The Old Testament Idea of God the Basis of Jesus' Teaching.

"Ye search the Scriptures because ye think that in them ye have eternal life; and these are they which bear witness of me" (John v. 39).

JESUS does not set forth a new divinity. He was not open to the specious charge laid against Socrates.

The Attitude of Jesus toward the Old Testament

On this point as elsewhere the Master rested his teaching concerning God the

Father on the Old Testament revelation. He does not hesitate to appeal to the Old Testament for a summary of duty to God and man under two commandments. "The first is, 'Hear, O Israel; The Lord our God, the Lord is one; and thou shalt love the Lord thy God with all thy heart, and with all thy soul, and with all thy mind, and with all thy strength.' The second is this, 'Thou shalt love thy neighbor as thyself.' There is none other commandment greater than these" (Mark xii. 29–31). In fact Jesus often chided the teachers of the time with ignorance of the Scriptures which they professed to teach (John v. 39), with ignorance of "the power of God" also (Matthew xxii. 29), and in particular with ignorance of the relation between the Messiah as the son of David and the Father (Matthew xxii. 42-45). So it is not a new God, but new light on the God of Israel that Jesus comes to present. It is just because he has a fresh and helpful message, a necessary word, about the God of the Old Testament that he speaks at all. "I came out from the Father and am come into the world" (John xvi. 28). "O righteous Father, the world knew thee not, but I knew thee; and these knew that thou didst send me; and I made known unto them thy name, and will make it known" (John xvii. 25 f.). Jesus here states the high purpose of his coming to earth, to manifest to men anew the God already known in part and, alas, forgotten in fact.

The Progressive Character of Old Testament Teaching about God

It was not to be expected that God would manifest himself fully at first. The Old Testament purports to be a faithful record of God's dealing with the race through a chosen people in getting them ready for the coming of his Son, the Messiah, who was to bring salvation to the lost. This view is here accepted as against the theory which makes the Old Testament merely a retrospect on the part of dreamers and idealists of Israel who wished to incite the people to better things by idealized and even fictitious pictures of the past that would flatter the nation's vanity and stimulate their hope. The acknowledgment that God had a definite, consistent and permanent purpose in this revelation does not preclude the freest and the fullest historical development. But the initiative and the control are placed with God in fact as well as in representation. In no other way can the integrity and value of the Old Testament be preserved; only thus can any really adequate explanation of the facts of Israelitish history be offered. Those who follow the other line of explanation do not hesitate to disregard the Old Testament facts that are inconsistent with the theory assumed to be true, a favorite method with dogmatic theologians of all shades of belief. If we may rearrange and set aside the facts in Israelitish history, we are free to adopt any theory that we please. It is time to speak a good word for the Old Testament, for it will survive the present storm. Jesus did not hesitate to use and appeal to the Old Testament. It seems needless to say that there is no polytheism in the Old Testament teaching, though much of it is found in the practice of the people. The Israelites are not alone in history as examples of those who knew and did not. The great lesson of Israelitish history is the lesson of monotheism. When they would not listen to prophetic teaching, they were turned over to the Assyrian, Babylonian and Persian rule. The exile burned the lesson into their very blood.

What is the Old Testament Teaching about God the Father

The God of Israel becomes the God of the nations under prophetic teaching.

The dominant notes of the Old Testament are the reality, the singleness, the power, the glory, the jealous love of God. Almost every act is represented as done in reference to God. The Old Testament saint walked "before God," "with God." He sinned "against God," "against the Lord." In history, prophecy, and psalm "the eternal God," "the most high God," "the God of heaven," "the holy God," "the God of hosts," "the Lord God of hosts," "the Lord of hosts," "the mighty God," "the Lord God of the fathers" is presented with terrible directness and awe-inspiring vividness. The supremacy and glory of God and the weakness of man stand out strongly in the Old Testament. Not often is God called "Father" in the Old Testament, and yet the fact and the idea are both present. In Jeremiah xxxi. 9, Jehovah says: "For I am a father to Israel, and Ephraim is my first-born." Likewise in Hosea xi. 1, Israel is called "my son" by Jehovah. All this is in the narrow sense of Father clearly as maintaining a peculiar relation to the people of his choice. In Malachi ii. 10, we read: "Have we not all one Father? Hath not our God created us?" Here the wider sense of "Father" is apparently applied to God, not merely as spiritual father of a peculiar people, but as creator of all men. However it is possible that even here the covenant idea dominates. In the Psalms we meet with the character of God as Father. So Psalm lxviii. 5: "A father of the fatherless, and a judge of widows, is God in his holy habitation." In Psalm ciii. 13 we read: "Like as a father pitieth his children, so Jehovah pitieth them that fear him." Clearly then the Old Testament has the basis for the teaching of the Son concerning his Father. The Old Testament has many names for God, as El, Elohim, Shaddai, El-Shaddai, El-Elyon, Jehovah. But it also has the name of Father, possibly in the general sense of creator and certainly in the particular sense of spiritual relationship to those who are thus bound to him by covenant ties.

The Character of God in the Old Testament

He is spirit and not matter. Many anthropomorphic expressions are used in the Old Testament about the emotions and the deeds of God, but these clearly are not designed to be taken literally. God is absolute righteousness. He is holy and just and good. He is unapproachable in ineffable glory, but condescends to manifest his presence through the Shekinah. He is thus ethical in nature, is in fact the basis of ethical conceptions. He is the cause of everything, animate and inanimate, physical and spiritual. He is a personal God, not a mere influence, not an idol, not the universe. He dwells everywhere and no one can escape his presence. He is "the living

God" and manifests the reality of his presence in many ways that suit his purposes. He is superhuman and all powerful, is Lord of nature and not the slave of his own laws. He can thunder at Sinai and he can speak at Horeb in the still small voice.

God's Covenant with Men

In nothing does the Old Testament unfold God as Father so clearly as in the covenant of grace, prompted by his love for sinners, put in definite shape in the promise to Abraham, repeated to David, and expounded in prophets and psalms. Hear Jehovah speaking to David concerning Solomon and the kingdom: "He shall build me an house and I will establish his throne forever. I will be his father and he shall be my son" (I Chron. xvii. 12 f.). The Messianic promise presents God as King in his kingdom, the everlasting spiritual kingdom (II Sam. vii. 13, 16; Ps. lxxxix. 3–5).

But God the Father in love offers his own Son as the priestly sacrifice for sin so wondrously outlined in Isaiah liii. The Old Testament had already told men of God the Father. What has Jesus more to say? Will he have a fuller and a final word about God?

CHAPTER III

Jesus the Revealer of God the Father to Men.

"He that hath seen me hath seen the Father" (John xiv. 9).

GOD is a person and cannot be clearly apprehended by abstract teaching. The Old Testament revelation was a progressive unfolding of the character of God with a promise of a richer revelation in the coming Messiah. The law was only the pedagogue that led the Jews to the great Teacher. Philosophy had failed to satisfy the spiritual aspirations of men, as they had failed to obey the moral law. Grace and truth, which came by Jesus (John i. 17) brought out the gentler side of the divine nature. Grace is the distinctive word of Christianity, but Christianity is more even than grace.

The Love of the Father Sends the Son

Behind the work and mission of Christ stands revealed in Christ the love of God, stated in the words of Jesus himself in all probability (though possibly the words of the evangelist John): "For God so loved the world, that he gave his only begotten Son, that whosoever believeth on him should not perish, but have eternal life" (John iii. 16). So then Jesus himself is the supreme proof of the love of the Father for the world. The testimony of the Gospel of John is here appealed to and will be used constantly on a par with that of the Synoptic Gospels. It is well known that some critics are unwilling to admit the historical character of the sayings of Jesus in John's Gospel who do admit those in the Synoptic Gospels. This is not the place to discuss that question, but ample grounds justify the use of all four Gospels as competent witnesses to the words of Jesus in historical exegesis, but with due perspective and proper apprehension of the relation of the Gospels to each other. Clearly then the motive of Christ's life is to fulfil the high mission of the Father in sending him to men. In fact the Master explicitly and repeatedly claims to voice the will of the Father. "We speak that which we know, and bear witness of that which we have seen" (John iii. 11). This he said to Nicodemus in justification of his right to teach the doctrine of the spiritual birth at which Nicodemus stumbled. In a summary of his teaching spoken at the very end and given in John xii. 44–50 Jesus closes thus: "For I spake not from myself; but the Father that sent me, he hath given me a commandment what I should say, and what I should speak. And I know that his commandment is life eternal; the things therefore which I speak, even as the Father hath said unto me, so I speak." In the synagogue at Capernaum Jesus distinctly claims that God has sent him to be the Messiah according to the prophecy of Isaiah (Luke iv. 18 f.).

Jesus Qualified to Reveal the Father

So Christ claimed and so he is. On the human side he was devoutly pious, had the clearest knowledge of the Old Testament teaching of God, and lived a life of close communion with the Father. But he needed more than this if he was to give the world the full and final revelation of God. A mere man could tell of God's dealings with him and others like him and could disclose the aspects of God's character into which he had gained insight by study, by communion with God, and by revelation from God.

But no mere man could manifest God to men in his eternal, absolute, and universal relations to men and at the same time bring him home to the hearts of men as a real person and as the loving and mighty Father. It is not strange, therefore, to find the evangelist John, who was the beloved disciple and who caught best the true character of Christ, saying of him: "And we beheld his glory, glory as of the only begotten from the Father" (John i. 14). This may be an allusion to the transfiguration scene, but John was no Docetic Gnostic, for he says also: "That which we have heard, that which we have seen with our eyes, that which we beheld, and our hands handled, concerning the Word of life . . . declare we unto you" (I John i. 1f.).

But this is not all. John makes the definite assertion of the pre-existence of the Word with the Father (John i. 1), "the Word was with God." This coexistence with the Father by the Word was eternal also, "in the beginning." No ideal pre-existence in the mind of the Father will satisfy the demands of this language nor the words of Jesus himself in John ix. 58: "Before Abraham was, I am." The term Word (Logos) is used in no mere philosophical sense either Platonic or Philonian, for "the Word became flesh, and dwelt among us" (John i. 14). Moreover, John has in mind the very point under discussion and speaks pointedly on it when he says: "No man hath seen God at any time: the only begotten Son, which is in the bosom of the Father, he hath declared him" (John i. 18). The best ancient documents here read "God only begotten" instead of "the only begotten Son," which would be a direct statement of the essential Godhead of Jesus. But whatever be the true reading John expressly asserts that "the Word was God" (John i. 1), and "the Word became flesh" (John i. 14). The Son "is in the bosom of the

Father," John says, signifying an eternal relationship. Hence he is fully able to manifest the Father to men. He is the Word of God and so "hath declared him" to men. The word rendered declare is in root our very word *exegesis*. In measured phrase, therefore, John asserts the eternal pre-existence of the Word, the existence of the Word with God, the identity of this Word with God, an identity not in person, but in essence and character for he is "in the bosom of the Father" and "hath declared him" when he "became flesh."

But it is not in John's Gospel alone that Jesus is thus presented as God. Matthew expressly explains the prophecy about the name Immanuel as meaning "God with us" (Matt. i. 23), and this not in a providential but a personal sense. In the temptations of Jesus Satan addressed him as "a Son of God" (no article with "Son" in the Greek, but with "God"). He was not willing to admit the full force of the testimony of the Father at the baptism when he called him "My beloved Son" (Mark i. 11). Jesus accepted worship from the disciples as the Son of God (Matt. xiv. 33), and this was in not simply a "religious value" sense, whatever the disciples at this time believed about Jesus, for they "worshipped" him.

The Claim of Jesus about his Message concerning the Father

Nothing is plainer than the high claims made by Jesus concerning his knowledge of the Father. In the next chapter the precise relation between the Father and the Son will be discussed at length. Just here we may properly present what the Master has to say about his own message. To the woman of Samaria at Jacob's well he said: "If thou knewest the gift of God, and who it is that saith to thee, Give me to drink; thou wouldst have asked of him, and he would have given thee living water" (John iv. 10). To the disciples, astonished that he did not eat the food which they had brought, he replied: "My meat is to do the will of him that sent me, and to accomplish his work" (John iv. 34). When the Pharisees from Jerusalem reasoned in their hearts that he was a blasphemer, Jesus said: "But that ye may know that the Son of man hath power on earth to forgive sins (he saith to the sick of the palsy), I say unto thee, Arise, take up thy bed, and go unto thy house" (Mark ii. 10 f.).

But not power alone did Jesus claim, power that put him on a level with the Father. Besides power he distinctly avows such knowledge of the Father as no one else possessed: "All things have been delivered unto me of my Father: and no one knoweth the Son, save the Father: neither doth any know the Father, save the Son, and he to whomsoever the Son willeth to reveal him" (Matt. xi. 27). Here the Son expressly asserts that the only way to know the Father is through the Son. The will of the Son decides to whom he will reveal the Father. This high claim is intolerant of rivalry. Not Zoroaster, not Buddha, not Confucius, not Mahomet, but Jesus alone reveals the Father to men. It is impossible to smooth down this absolute claim, for it is supported by the whole tenor of the teaching of Jesus, especially in the Gospel of John. These words in Matthew, repeated also at a later time (see Luke x. 22), reinforce the historical reality of the Johannine teaching. Neither the Unitarian nor the Ritschlian view of Jesus is consonant with the claims of equality with God here made by Christ. So the Lord Jesus urges men, in order to come to knowledge of the Father, to come to himself. "Come unto me," says he, "take my yoke upon you, and learn of me" (Matt. xi. 28 f.).

In fact, Jesus refuses recognition in heaven before the Father to those who deny the Son here. "Every one therefore who shall confess me before men, him will I also confess before my Father which is in heaven. But whosoever shall deny me before men, him will I also deny before my Father which is in heaven" (Matt. x. 32 f.). No more divine assumption of authority in the sphere of the spiritual life is possible than this. The way to the Father's presence is by the approval of the Son. This vital identity between the Father and the Son Jesus announced to the Galilean multitude in the synagogue at Capernaum at the climax of the Galilean ministry, and the announcement repelled the unspiritual populace who revolted at the spiritual conception of the Messiah. Jesus claimed to be "the true bread of God" (John vi. 32 f.), "the true bread out of heaven." When they murmured, Jesus replied: "No one can come to me, except the Father which sent me draw him" (John vi. 44), insisting again that he alone had "seen the Father" (John vi. 46). As they grew angry, Jesus went still further: "As the living Father sent me, and I live because of the Father: so he that eateth me, he also shall live because of me" (John vi. 57). As no one can come to the Father except by the Son, so no one can come to the Son "except it be given unto him of the Father" (John vi. 65). It is no wonder that under such a severe sifting the multitude melted away and left Jesus in the synagogue with the twelve. But the Father in heaven had revealed to Simon Peter that Jesus was the Messiah as he now and afterwards confessed (Matt. xvi. 16 f.).

If Jesus claimed to bear witness of the Father, he contended also that to reject him was displeasing to the Father, "He that rejecteth me rejecteth him that sent me" (Luke x. 16). If he bore witness of the Father, so the Father bore witness of him. "And the Father which sent me, he hath borne witness of me"

(John v. 37). At the baptism (Matt. iii. 11), the Father spoke approval of his mission. So was it also at the transfiguration (Mark ix. 7) and, when the Greeks came to him, the Father spoke audible cheer (John xii. 28). To his enemies therefore Jesus boldly claimed: "I am not alone, but I and the Father that sent me" (John viii. 16). When they sneeringly asked him, "Where is thy Father?" his reply was ready: "Ye know neither me nor my Father: if ye knew me, ye would know my Father also" (John viii. 19).

It is no wonder then that Jesus expresses surprise at the dulness of Thomas, saying: "I am the way, and the truth, and the life: no one cometh unto the Father, but by me. If ye had known me, ye would have known my Father also: from henceforth ye know him, and have seen him" (John xiv. 6 f.). The very climax of the self-revelation of the Father in the Son, as claimed by Christ, comes in his reply to Philip's sceptical appeal that he "shew us the Father." Hear the earnest plea of Jesus: "Have I been so long time with you, and dost thou not know me, Philip? He that hath seen me hath seen the Father; how sayest thou, Show us the Father? Believest thou not that I am in the Father, and the Father in me?" (John xiv. 9 f.). In these words the Son expresses the core of the great truth that he is the Revealer to men of God the Father. Henceforth men are without excuse who do not know the Father, for he has so expressed himself in the Son that all men may see and know. The Father and the Son really abide in the believer: "We will come and make our abode with him" (John xiv. 23).

The Character of God according to the Message of the Son

If Jesus is so well qualified to tell men the truth about God, as the Evangelists say and as *he himself* says, what then is his message? What has he to say? We now come to the heart of the subject of this book. The succeeding chapters aim to discuss in detail the various aspects of the message of Jesus concerning God the Father. But just here let us get a forecast of the whole treatment by a brief glance at the general features of the subject.

The first positive word that the Master spoke concerning the character of the Father, as given in the Gospels, is this: "God is a Spirit" or perhaps better "God is spirit" (John iv. 24). This clear word he spoke to the poor Samaritan woman who sought to inveigle the Saviour into a discussion of the theological controversy between the Jews and the Samaritans as to the true place of worship, whether Jerusalem or Gerizim. "They that worship him must worship in spirit and truth," "neither in this mountain, nor in Jerusalem, shall ye worship the Father," he said. These luminous words stand out in bold relief against the narrow and unspiritual conception of both Jew and Gentile. They remain yet the last and highest message about the nature of God. The world to-day, after dallying with materialism, is coming back to just this conception, that spirit is before matter, that life is spirit, and that the life of the world is God. As spirit God must be approached by the spirit. This then is the essence of worship, and not the form nor the place. The reality of worship rises above sacrament, ritual, place, as God is eternal spirit.

Another distinctive word that Jesus uses of God is Father. The word is in the Old Testament and is applied to God, but it remained for the Son to familiarize men with the term and the idea. It is on the lips of Jesus at every turn. "The Father," he says, or "My Father," "your Father," "our Father," or simply "Father," "Abba, Father." There is a difference in the relations expressed by these terms which will be brought out later. But he taught his disciples to say "Our Father" when they prayed (Matt. vi. 9). He taught the Fatherhood of God in a real and blessed sense. He made men feel that God is near and watches over them.

One other general idea of God Jesus presented. He insisted on the absolute goodness of God. The eager young ruler, who lightly addressed Jesus as "good Master," was quickly reminded that "none is good save one, even God" (Luke xviii. 19). This he did not to disclaim his own divinity, but to caution the young man and to pierce his idea of God and Christ. This is a needed lesson for all times. God is good. God is good to us, always good to us.

The power of God is without measure, Jesus taught. "All things are possible with God" (Mark x. 27). His disciples were distressed at the hard teaching of Jesus about the rich. If the rich had such a difficult task, who then can be saved? The difficulty is real, and the Master did not minimize it. He rather admitted the hopelessness of the situation from the point of view of men. But there is a higher way of seeing things. "With God all things are possible" (Matt. xix. 26).

Once more God is the God of the living, says Jesus. "God is not the God of the dead, but of the living" (Matt. xxii. 32). He is the living God himself and is the God of the living. This is an argument to show that the dead rise again, but it is also a definite message to the effect that God is living. In a word then, as Jesus speaks the message, God is the living God, God is spirit, God is good, God is the Father, God is all powerful, and God loves the world. Spiritual life, absolute holiness, endless power, and perfect love are the attributes that distinguish him that Jesus called and taught us to call Father. To love God, to trust God, to walk with God, to find God here, to go to God at last through the portal of death—this is eternal life, this is the true destiny of man.

Jesus in his prayer before his passion says: "And this is life eternal, that they should know thee, the only true God, and him whom thou didst send, even Jesus Christ" (John xvii. 3). He is fully conscious of the solemnity of his relation to men as the Revealer of the Father. He has not been able to make all men see Him, but he has helped the disciples to that end: "I manifested thy name unto the men whom thou gavest me out of the world" (John xvii. 6). He has this consolation then as he enters the shadow of the cross.

CHAPTER IV

The Relation of the Father to the Son.

"Thou art my beloved Son; in thee I am well pleased." Luke iii. 22. The Father to the Son.

"For thou lovedst me before the foundation of the world." John xvii. 24. The Son to the Father.

THE Evangelist John opens his Gospel with the statement in effect that the Logos eternally coexisted with God and was God. He continues in i. 18 and calls him "the only begotten Son, which is in the bosom of the Father." "And the Word became flesh and dwelt among us" (John i. 14).

The Unique Relation between the Father and the Son

This is most assuredly true. Jesus is called "the only begotten Son" also in John iii. 16, 18, where it is not clear whether we have the words of Jesus himself or the witness of the Evangelist. The angel Gabriel foretold to Mary that her Son should "be called the Son of the Most High" (Luke i. 32) and that the Lord God should "give unto him the throne of his father David," and "of his kingdom there should be no end" (Luke i. 32 f.). And to Mary's protest he replied: "The holy thing which is begotten shall be called the Son of God" (Luke i. 35). Thus both the human nature and the divine nature of the Christ are asserted by John the evangelist in retrospect and by the angel Gabriel in prophecy. Did Jesus himself realize such a peculiar relationship toward both God and men? In particular was he conscious of his Messianic mission and of a peculiar connection with God the Father? In seeking to learn the relation of the Father to the Son we are compelled to use the words of Jesus about that relation. In three instances alone do we have the direct words of the Father about the Son, but these are full of significance and strongly reinforce what the Son affirms. As Jesus entered upon his public ministry and came up out of the baptismal water, the Father spoke in audible voice, audible to the Son certainly, and said: "Thou art my beloved Son: in thee I am well pleased" (Mark i. 11). Here sonship of a special character is distinctly asserted by the Father. The words "my beloved" mark him off from other "sons of God" and the "good pleasure" is more absolute than that expressed about believers merely (Luke ii. 14) although the same word is used in both cases.

This testimony was at the introduction of the Messiah to his work. In the last year of the public ministry, when the Galilean ministry, like the earlier Judean, had resulted in the alienation of the people through jealousy of the leaders and lack of spiritual perception among the masses, the Saviour is facing his death. On the transfiguration mount the Father once more calls him "my beloved Son" (Matt. xvii. 5). In the last week of Christ's public work the message of the Greeks greatly agitates the heart of Jesus. They will come to him only by his death. He has real agony before Gethsemane and cries out: "Father, save me from this hour." But he instantly adds: "Father, glorify thy name." The Father heard this appeal and replied in audible voice understood by him though not clearly by the multitude: "I have both glorified it, and will glorify it again" (John xii. 27 f.). For the rest we must first see the Father through the Son's person and message. Thus we can gain a point of view by which we may form some adequate conception of the interrelation that subsists between the Father and the Son.

Jesus early became conscious that he was the Son of God in a special way. How soon the Messianic consciousness dawned in his mind we do not know, nor how fully he at first grasped the great fact in his life. That he grew "in favor with God and men" (Luke ii. 52) we do know. When first "the boy Jesus" emerges out of the obscurity of the silent years at Nazareth, the boy of twelve left in Jerusalem by Joseph and Mary, he exhibits knowledge of his unique position in the world. "Knew ye not that I must be in my Father's house?" he pleaded, when they expressed surprise at finding him there. He describes God as "my Father," whether we read "house" or "business." He has already come into the consciousness of his real self. By "my

Father" he meant more than by "our Father."

The words "my Father" are often on his lips in after years. The first time that the Messiah appears in Jerusalem after his baptism, he boldly asserts authority over the temple and drives the money changers and market venders out. "Make not," said he, "my Father's house a house of merchandise" (John ii. 16). It was his Father's house in a sense that was not true of mere worshipers of God. When the Jews in Jerusalem find fault with Jesus for having healed the impotent man on the Sabbath day, he says: "My Father worketh even until now, and I work" (John v. 17). The effect of this claim was instantaneous. "The Jews sought the more to kill him, because he not only broke the Sabbath, but also called God his own Father, making himself equal with God" (John v. 18). It will not do to say that the Jews here misunderstood the claims of Jesus as to his unique relation to the Father, for he proceeded at once to prove the high claims of equality with the Father. It is not necessary to prove by further exegetical remark from the use of the phrase "my Father" the uniqueness of the relation between the Father and the Son. Let a few quotations suffice. "All things have been delivered unto me of my Father" (Matt. xi. 27); "My Father giveth you the true bread out of heaven" (John vi. 32); "For flesh and blood hath not revealed it unto thee, but my Father who is in heaven" (Matt. xvi. 17); "In heaven their angels do always behold the face of my Father who is in heaven" (Matt. xviii. 10); "But I honor my Father, and ye dishonor me" (John viii. 49). These are representative sayings of Jesus in which he calls God "my Father."

It is impossible to say that here Jesus merely claimed God as his Father in the same sense that any other child of God has the right to do. To his enemies he said: "Ye have not known him: but I know him; and if I should say I know him not, I shall be like you, a liar"(John viii. 55). He insists on this unique relationship in the face of bitter denial.

Often Christ speaks of God as "the Father." This usage is almost confined to the Gospel of John where it is very common, while "my Father" is common in all the Gospels. In John "the Father" is sometimes God in relation to his children in general, though even here in contrast to the Son as in John v. 23: "That all may honour the Son, even as they honour the Father." Usually, however, in John's Gospel, the expression "the Father" in the mouth of Jesus represents God in his relation to the Son, as "the Father loveth the Son" (John v. 20), "even as the Father knoweth me and I know the Father" (John x. 15), "because I go to the Father" (John xvi. 10). The Father and the Son are often mentioned together in the discourses of Christ in the Gospel of John. The passage in Matt. xi. 29–30 (cf. also Luke x. 22), which is so much like the words of Christ in the Fourth Gospel, has likewise "the Father" and "the Son" in mutual relationship of utmost intimacy.

Sometimes, as in prayer, Jesus says simply "Father." In Luke x. 21 he prays: "I thank thee, O Father, Lord of heaven and earth," and he goes on in the same verse, "yea, Father, for so it was well-pleasing in thy sight," though here the Greek has the article with the vocative. Beside the grave of Lazarus Christ spoke with confident trust: "Father, I thank thee that thou heardest me" (John xi. 41). In the Garden of Gethsemane Jesus cried out to God: "Father, if thou be willing" (Luke xxii. 42), "Abba, Father" (Mark xiv. 36) in the language of childhood in both Aramaic and Greek (with the article with each). On the cross he prayed: "Father, forgive them"

(Luke xxiii. 34), a disputed passage, but most probably genuine. He died with the utterance of these words: "Father, into thy hands I commend my spirit" (Luke xxiii. 46). In a world of hypocrisy and religiosity Jesus stood in lonely and lofty purity and sincerity. He found full fellowship of spirit only with the Father and the Holy Spirit. His heart beat in compassion for men and in sympathy with men, but at the same time he stood apart from men. His highest and holiest communion was with the Father whose only begotten Son he was. If this was true, more was true.

What is the Relation between Father and Son in Nature

Has the Father given to the Son in actual being what his other children do not possess? It is sometimes said that evolution brings Christ under inevitable law and makes it impossible for him to differ in nature from other men, however far he excels them in character. But even on scientific grounds Jesus is the grand exception in the race, unless we deny the records that we have about his career. Those who revolt at the superhuman, not to say supernatural, calmly brush aside the Gospel accounts as discredited, but then the supreme character remains. It was drawn by somebody. The story of the virgin birth is thrust into the limbo of the legendary. But what then becomes of Christ? Whose Son is he? This very question the Master pressed home to his enemies after their complete rout on the last day of his teaching in the temple. If he is merely "the Son of David" and so merely human, "how then doth David in the Spirit call him Lord?" (Matt. xxii. 42 f.) On the other hand, "If David then calleth him Lord" and so he is only divine, "how is he his son?" (Matt. xxii. 45.) "No one was able to answer him a word" then, nor can any one solve that riddle now who does not admit the real humanity and the real divinity of Jesus Christ. It is no mere official relation nor does Jesus simply have the religious value of God's Son. The relation is vital and eternal.

It is true that Jesus urges those who follow him to "be one; even as thou, Father, art in me, and I in thee" (John xvii. 20 f.), "that they may be one, even as we are" (John xvii. 11). But none the less the Son insists on a real difference between the relation of the Son and the disciples and that of the Son and the Father. "And now, Father, glorify thou me with thine own self with the glory which I had with thee before the world was" (John xvii. 5). Here he isolates the Father and himself apart from the world and before there was a world, when he was with the Father's "own self." Ideal pre-existence is inconceivable in this passage. We may not penetrate the mysteries of the divine essence, but here

Father and Son are set apart from all the world in being and glory and are on a plane of perfect equality that is incomprehensible save on the understanding that Jesus is in very nature the Son of God. It is only as we perceive this fact that we can give hearty respect to one who made such claims about himself as Jesus did. With this frank admission there is no discord when he says: "I am the way, and the truth, and the life: no one cometh unto the Father, but by me" (John xiv. 6). Thus he is able to "shew us the Father" because he is able truthfully to say: "I am in the Father, and the Father in me" (John xiv. 11). So we can be brought into contact with the Father, "I in them and thou in me" (John xvii. 23).

It is not surprising then to hear Jesus call himself "the Son of God" as he does a few times. This is the constant implication of the words so often on his lips, "my Father," "the Father," "the Son."

In the early part of the ministry at the second visit to Jerusalem he was accused by the Jews of calling "God his own Father" and "making himself equal with God." So far from denying this charge he even said in defence: "The hour cometh, and now is, when the dead shall hear the voice of the Son of God; and they that hear shall live" (John v. 25). When Lazarus was at the point of death, Jesus boldly declared that this sickness was "for the glory of God, that the Son of God may be glorified thereby" (John xi. 4). But most of all, when put on oath by the high priest at his trial before the Sanhedrin, Jesus asserted expressly that he was the Son of God: "I adjure thee by the living God, that thou tell us whether thou be the Christ, the Son of God. Jesus saith unto him, Thou hast said" (Matt. xxvi. 63 f.). Mark represents Jesus as saying in reply simply: "I am" (Mark xiv. 62).

It seems clear from this what the Jews

understood Christ to mean by the expression "the Son of God." At any rate his own teachings make clear what he meant to claim. In view of all that is true, it is rather surprising to find the words "the Son of God" used so little by the Master. Perhaps he avoided it partly because of possible political consequences as he usually avoided the use of "Messiah" for the same reason. It is not to be replied that Jesus claimed to be God only in the sense true of those who were given authority by God. He used this argument (John x. 34–36). "Is it not written in your law, I said, Ye are gods?" in rebuttal of the charge that he was guilty of blasphemy, "because that thou, being a man, makest thyself God" (John x. 33). He had just said: "I and the Father are one" (John x. 30). He did not deserve the charge of blasphemy even if he was only a god in the lower sense, by no means admitting that this was all the truth. The term therefore is personal, expressing his relation to God, as well as official and Messianic.

Jesus did claim his special divine Sonship when it was wise or necessary, but he rejoiced to assert his humanity. The phrase "the Son of man" is ever in his mouth. This expression cannot be whittled down to mean merely "a man." It had a Messianic significance, though perhaps not generally so understood, and was pre-eminently fitting for him who was in every sense the ideal man, the representative man of all time. The very pregnancy of the term makes it all the more suitable. He used the words "the Son of man" not only when speaking of his earthly work, but when discussing his power and glory, as when he replied to the question of the high priest at the trial before the Sanhedrin: "Henceforth ye shall see the Son of man sitting at the right hand of power, and coming on the clouds of heaven" (Matt. xxvi. 64). There is nothing to justify us in speaking of the divinity of Christ in distinction from the deity of the Father. This is a Ritschlian refinement foreign to the teaching of the Gospels. John said expressly: "The Word was God" (John i. 1).

The Father and Son have an Interflow of Knowledge

Jesus was a man and grew in knowledge. But he also was God and the Father's will and word came richly to him in ways not true of mere men. "For the Father loveth the Son, and sheweth him all things that himself doeth" (John v. 20). Once more in the same great discourse Jesus said: "As I hear, I judge; and . . . I seek not mine own will, but the will of him that sent me" (John v. 30). When the hostile Jews marvelled at the source of his teaching, since he had not their scholastic training, Jesus said simply: "My teaching is not mine, but his that sent me" (John vii.

16). By the open grave of Lazarus Christ in calm trust looked up to God and said: "Father, I thank thee that thou heardest me" (John xi. 41), adding: "And I knew that thou hearest me always." Jesus claimed to be the absolute teacher of righteousness by reason of his relation to the Father.

And yet he had some limitations in his knowledge. He himself said of the day of his second coming: "But of that day or that hour knoweth no one, not even the angels in heaven, neither the Son, but the Father" (Mark xiii. 32). Why Christ had superhuman knowledge and yet was astonished at the faith of some and the doubt of others we cannot tell. The mind of Christ is part of the mystery of his person. But we may reverently assert that what he did teach was authoritative and final. He taught no error, though he did not teach everything. He is the final authority where he does speak, for he speaks the will of the

Father. In the darkness of the cross, Jesus cried out: "My God, my God, why hast thou forsaken me?" (Matt. xxvii. 46). Here the frown of the Father rested on the Son as he died for our sins; he was looked on as sin indeed. How the Father, when one in nature with the Son, could thus forsake the Son we do not venture to discuss.

The Father and the Son Work in Harmony

There is no self-will in the Son toward the Father. He gladly claims union with the Father in nature, knowledge, and power. "The Son can do nothing of himself, but what he seeth the Father doing" (John v. 19). And this is not mere imitation as earthly children copy the deeds of their parents. "For as the Father hath life in himself, even so gave he to the Son also to have life in himself" (John v. 26). With such power and rank the Master dares to claim for himself honor like that of the Father: "That all may honor the Son, even as they honor the Father. He that honoreth not the Son honoreth not the Father which sent him" (John v. 23 f.). This he said to the hostile Jews in Jerusalem who protested against his "making himself equal with God."

No mere man could soberly say what Matthew represents Christ as saying after the message from John the Baptist: "All things have been delivered unto me of my Father" (Matt. xi. 27). This supreme authority Jesus often asserted. Even as he entered into the dark hours of the Passion Week, he walked steadily on, John says, "Knowing that the Father had given all things into his hands" (John xiii. 3). After his resurrection from the grave, the once homeless teacher boldly uttered a cry of victory as he sent a band of disciples on a world conquest: "All authority hath been given unto me in heaven and in earth" (Matt. xxviii. 18). Satan had offered him power on earth for the price of a bow of worship, but now the Master has power assured in heaven and earth.

The Father and the Son are One in Character

In the nature of the case Christ would say little about being as holy as God the Father. Once in fact when a rich young ruler came to him and called him "Good Master," Jesus questioned his use of the adjective "good" in reference to himself. "Why callest thou me good? None is good save one, even God" (Mark x. 18). But we do not here understand Christ to deny that he is good, as some say, but only to assert absolute goodness of God alone from the ruler's point of view. The young man doubtless did not take Christ to be divine, as he is in reality. Hence he needed care in the use of the word "good." The very caution of Christ here serves to set in relief his own character. He is good as God is good.

We also think of Jesus as the expression of God's goodness. In this sense God is as good as Jesus. This is the verdict of men, practically of all men. No adjectives are used to picture the life of Jesus in the Gospels. He himself says nothing about his personal character save as we gather it in hints and deeds. But his character is distinct and clear cut. If to see Jesus was to see the Father, then is Jesus like the Father in spirit and life. This Christ claimed for himself: "If ye had known me, ye would have known my Father also" (John xiv. 7). But the Father called him his "beloved Son" and expressed good pleasure in him (Matt. iii. 17). We have been treading on holy ground as we have sought to unfold the relation between the Father and the Son. He joyfully confessed: "My Father is greater than I" (John xiv. 28). He is speaking of office, but they are one in nature, knowledge, power, and character. The eternal Father and the eternal Son are also one in love for a lost and ruined world.

The Apologetic of Jesus

Perhaps a paragraph should be added for the purpose of calling attention to the great number of Christ's sayings about the relation between the Father and himself. He speaks far more about this aspect of the Father's revelation than about any other. There are obvious reasons for this fact. For one thing it was a necessary introduction to his right to speak so full and free a message from the Father. His high claim to peculiar oneness with the Father could not be taken on his mere statement. This Jesus freely admitted, though insisting that his words were true even if they were not accepted on his affirmation. In a true sense Christ was on the defensive before his enemies, and when attacked for making himself equal with God, he had to enter into extended discussion of the holy relation subsisting between the Father and the Son. This is seen especially at the feast in Jerusalem (John v.), at the feast of tabernacles (John vii. 7–x. 21), at the feast of dedication (John x. 22–42).

In the farewell discourse to the disciples in the upper room just before his death Christ opened his heart to them and spoke frankly of the Father, the Holy Spirit, and himself (John xii–xvii.). This passage in John is the holy of holies of the teaching of Jesus. And then besides Christ had come into the world to manifest the Father, to win the world back to the Father. It is natural therefore that he should speak often of his own relation to the Father in the execution of his high mission. All else is after the King. The great, the supreme message of Jesus is the revelation that he offers in himself of God the Father. If he speaks less at length about other relations of the Father, we must remember that in Christ God is reconciling the world to himself.

The Father's Satisfaction in the Son

We are under necessity to be cautious in all that we say concerning the emotions of God the Father. But he thrice spoke audibly his good pleasure in the person and work of the Son, as has already been shown, at the baptism, at the transfiguration, and when the Greeks came to seek Jesus. The Son came forth from the Father, and went back to the Father: "I came out from the Father . . . and go unto the Father" (John xvi. 28). But all during his earthly ministry the Father was with him: "and yet I am not alone, because the Father is with me" (John xvi. 32). He never doubted the confidence that the Father had in him. When he faced his death, he calmly prayed: "Father, the hour is come; glorify thy Son, that the Son may glorify thee" (John xvii. 2). He could give his disciples no greater measure of his love for them than the Father's love for him: "Even as the Father hath loved me, I also have loved you" (John xv. 9). He was doing what he did "that the world may know that I love the Father" (John xiv. 31).

In the Garden of Gethsemane he did not incur the Father's displeasure, for he only asked that the cup pass, "Father, if thou be willing" (Luke xxii. 42). And even as on the cross the Son cried out that the Father had forsaken him, yet it was for this very purpose that the Father had sent him into the world. "For God so loved the world that he gave his only begotten Son, that whosoever believeth on him should not perish, but have eternal life" (John iii. 16). The heart of Christ was torn with grief at the thought of separation from his disciples, but he ventured to say that, if they really knew what it meant for them and for him that he go, they would not grieve.

"If ye loved me, ye would have rejoiced, because I go unto the Father" (John xiv. 28). Henceforth he "is in the bosom of the Father" (John i. 18). But the Father is forever nearer to us and we come, as Thomas did, and say to Jesus, "My Lord and my God" (John xx. 28). Jesus told Mary Magdalene to say to the disciples for him: "I ascend unto my Father and your Father, and my God and your God" (John xx. 17). So we draw near to the Father, for Jesus in heaven is the God-man still, our Brother and Friend, our God and Saviour.

CHAPTER V

The Relation of the Father to the Holy Spirit.

"And I will pray the Father and he shall give you anothe Comforter, that he may be with you for ever, even the Spirit of truth." (John xiv. 16).

WE are not here concerned with metaphysical speculations.

The Fact of the Trinity

There is no technical discussion of the Trinity in the New Testament. But the fact is clearly revealed in various parts of the Scriptures. The Gospels form no exception. If we had no knowledge of the Holy Spirit, the teaching of Jesus would make necessary a dual God. His own deity is indubitable. However, a Triune God is the manifest unfolding of Christ. If he reveals the Father, he also declares his equality with the Father. If he claims deity for himself, he also asserts the deity of the Holy Spirit. Jesus does not give a detailed discussion of the nature of the Trinity. But the essential fact revealed is that God is one: "The Lord our God, the Lord is one" (Mark xii. 29). This is not a new revelation, for the Old Testament is uniformly monotheistic in teaching and Jesus here is quoting the Old Testament.

But beside this cardinal fact in the teaching of Christ lies the other fact of his own deity and that of the Holy Spirit. We may not be able to state in scientific formula the idea of the Trinity. Three Persons in one nature may seem intangible to us. Be it so. We must discriminate sharply between the fact of the Trinity and theories about the Trinity. What Christ reveals is not a mere modal Trinity. It is not that God manifests himself now as Father, now as Son, now as Holy Spirit. The rather all three Persons co-exist in the one essence and co-work in the salvation of men. Humility well becomes us all in applying to the infinite Godhead the metes and bounds of our finite reason. Christ himself is sufficient guarantee for the truth that he reveals even if it is incomprehensible to our mind. He is the truth and can speak only the truth. We may rest in him.

Jesus himself under the Spirit's Guidance in his Earthly Life

The very birth of Jesus illustrates the intimate and vital union of the three Persons in the Godhead. The angel said to Mary that Jesus was to be begotten of the Holy Spirit: "The Holy Spirit shall come upon thee, and the power of the Most High shall overshadow thee" (Luke i. 35), and he is to be God's Son for this very reason: "Wherefore also the holy thing which is begotten shall be called the Son of God" (ibid.). At the baptism of Jesus likewise the Father audibly expressed his approval of the Son while the Holy Spirit appeared in bodily form like a dove and rested on Jesus (Luke iii. 22). It is not here claimed that this significant event explains clearly the relations that subsist in the Trinity, but only the vital reality and close connection of Father, Son, and Spirit. We may not say that Jesus was not under the guidance of the Holy Spirit before this time, but simply that now in a formal manner as he enters upon his public Messianic mission the Father and the Spirit set the seal of their approval upon him.

It is beyond dispute that Jesus in his earthly life was under the control of the Holy Spirit as well as in subjection to the will of the Father. Jesus was led of the Spirit into the wilderness (Matt. iv. 1), and in the temptation there the Spirit was with him. In his first sermon at Nazareth he said: "The Spirit of the Lord is upon me" (Luke iv. 18). He maintained that he wrought his miracles by the Spirit of God (Matt. xii. 28), though evidently with no reflection on the power of the Father nor of his own power. The way in which the divine power worked in him in the case of the miracles was by the Spirit. We need not assert that Christ did not draw upon his own divine power. To do so would lay too much stress upon the difference between Father, Son, and Spirit. Jesus lived the life of God: "My meat is to do the will of him that sent me" (John iv. 34); and in full fellowship of the Holy Spirit: "In that same hour he rejoiced in the Holy Spirit, and said, I thank thee, O Father" (Luke x. 21). So reads the correct text here.

The Holy Spirit a Person in the Same Sense that the Father is a Person

It is necessary at least to call attention to this important fact, since some Christians fail to perceive it. The passages just quoted concerning the birth and life of Jesus bear witness to the distinct personality of the Holy Spirit. The Spirit is not merely the power of God or the influence of God. Father, Son, and Spirit are repeatedly mentioned together on the same plane of personal reality. In the discourses in the upper room (John xiii–xvii.), Jesus many times assumes the personal existence of the Holy Spirit in as true a sense as he himself existed. Let one quotation suffice: "But the Comforter, even the Holy Spirit, whom the Father will send in my name, he shall teach you all things" (John xiv. 26). In the Great Commission Jesus sends forth the disciples to baptize "in the name of the Father and of the Son and of the Holy Ghost" (Matt. xxviii. 19). The teaching of Christ is clear on this subject.

The Order of the Persons in the Trinity

In his earthly career the Son is under the guidance of the Holy Spirit, but the other facts given seem clearly to show that this is not the normal situation. We hesitate to lay special emphasis on such a point as this, for, of course, in the order of the Godhead there is perfect harmony as well as identity of essence. And yet when the three are spoken of together it is usually in the order of Father, Son, and Spirit. And more than this, the Son himself asserts an order of rank over the Spirit in one respect: "But when the Comforter is come, whom I will send unto you from the Father, even the Spirit of truth, which proceedeth from the Father, he shall bear witness of me" (John xv. 26). In John xiv. 26, he had said: "whom the Father will send in my name." Moreover, after the resurrection Jesus "breathed on them and saith unto them, Receive ye the Holy Spirit" (John xx. 22). Jesus said: "The Father is greater than I" (John xiv. 28). In point of rank therefore it seems clear that there is a difference in the Trinity.

But the Son "is in the bosom of the Father," and the Holy Spirit, Jesus said, "shall glorify me; for he shall take of mine, and shall declare it unto you" (John xvi. 14). Moreover, the Holy Spirit "shall not speak from himself; but whatsoever things he shall hear, these shall he speak" (John xvi. 13). As the Son on earth spoke for the Father, so the Holy Spirit would speak from the Father and reveal the Son to men. The Son came to manifest the Father to the world in himself. The Spirit would come to reveal to men the Son and thus the Father. As the Son glorified the Father, so the Spirit would glorify the Son. As the Son owed his birth to the Holy Spirit, so men would become children of God by the Spirit, though to be sure in a different sense than is true of Jesus. We despair of any effort to put in intelligible form the basal and eternal facts of the glorious Trinity, but none the less we reverently and joyfully accept God as revealed by Christ as Father, Son, and Spirit. This is more than an economic or a metaphysical Trinity. But we do not have three separate Gods. Christianity is not polytheistic. Electricity is light, heat, and power. Radium bids us all to be slow to say dogmatically what cannot be true in the realm of the eternal.

Blasphemy against the Holy Spirit is Blasphemy against God

Jesus would not brook an insult to his Father nor to the Holy Spirit. The Pharisees were not able to deny the reality of the miracles of Jesus, but in desperation they attributed them to Satan, accusing Jesus of being in league with the devil. They hoped thus to offset the effect of his works. But Jesus boldly claimed to work them by the Spirit of God (Matt. xii. 28), and accused them of blasphemy against the Holy Spirit, which sin is eternal and has no forgiveness (Mark iii. 29 f.). In fact Jesus held blasphemy against the Holy Spirit to be worse than blasphemy against the Son: "And whosoever shall speak a word against the Son, it shall be forgiven him; but whosoever shall speak against the Holy Spirit, it shall not be forgiven him" (Matt. xii. 32). This is true not because the Holy Spirit is greater than the Son, but because there was less excuse for it. The Son of man was in human form, and perhaps more excuse was possible when he was treated as a mere man. But the Holy Spirit was not man at all, but God alone, and the works thus manifestly wrought by the Spirit of God were diabolically attributed to Satan. It was the climax of malevolence, when the very works of God, and plain works of God, were credited to the power of Satan. This is indeed a *lèse majesté* in the highest sense of that term. The full deity and the real personality of the Holy Spirit are implied in the teaching of Christ concerning the unpardonable sin. It is not hard to see the justice of this hard penalty. The depth of the iniquity of the Pharisees is thus apprehended against whom Jesus later let loose the vials of his just wrath (Matt. xxiii.).

The Promise of the Father to Send the Spirit

We are not to think that the Holy Spirit was not in the world at all before the day of Christ. No more are we to say that God had no kingdom on earth before John the Baptist proclaimed the advent of the kingdom of God. In a new sense the kingdom came with the coming of Christ, as in a new sense it will be fully come when Christ comes again to claim his own. So in a new and richer sense the Holy Spirit was to come when Jesus went back to the Father, although before that day Jesus had said that the heavenly Father would "give the Holy Spirit to them that ask him" (Luke xi. 13). He had also previously spoken of the coming of the Holy Spirit as "rivers of living water" "which they that believed on him were to receive" (John vii. 39 f.). John adds this also: "For the Spirit was not yet given," referring to the day of Pentecost. He wrote at the close of the century and was looking back to the great day when the Spirit of God began a new era in Christianity.

To the distressed disciples Jesus promised a Comforter who should be with them when he was gone: "And I will pray the Father, and he shall give you another Comforter, that he may be with you forever" (John xiv. 16). In fact, said Jesus, "if I go not away, the Comforter will not come unto you" (John xvi. 7), "but," he adds, "if I go, I will send him unto you," thus identifying his work with that of the Father.

At Jerusalem before the ascension, Jesus repeated the promise of the Father in specific terms: "And behold I send forth the promise of the Father upon you" (Luke xxiv. 49), adding: "Ye shall receive power, when the Holy Spirit is come upon you" (Acts i. 8). Clearly then the Holy Spirit was to take up the work of the Son and to carry it on to the end. But we are not to think of a merely absentee Christ who has withdrawn to the glory of heaven. He is at the right hand of the Father as our High Priest, Advocate, and Elder Brother, who pleads our cause on high with the Father while the Holy Spirit is Christ's advocate on earth with men. Indeed through the Holy Spirit Jesus is with us "always, even unto the end of the world" (Matt. xxviii. 20). So then all three Persons of the Trinity are actively engaged in the work of redemption.

It is possible in a general way to speak of the Old Testament dispensation as that of God the Father, the dispensation in the Gospels as that of Jesus the Son of God and the Son of man, and the apostolic dispensation as that of the Holy Spirit. But this can be said only by way of accent, not of separate work. For the Holy Spirit is not ignored in the Old Testament and the coming of the Messiah is the one great hope that lights up the Old Testament times. In the ministry of Jesus the supreme fact is the full revelation of God the Father in the Son while he himself is in constant communion with the Spirit. When the Son returned to the bosom of the Father, the Holy Spirit is in control of the kingdom of heaven on earth, and yet the chief work of the Holy Spirit is to make effective the work of the Son on the basis of whose atoning death it is possible for men to come back to God the Father. The Spirit, then, is the Father's ever-present Messenger who convicts "the world in respect of sin, and of righteousness, and of judgment" (John xvi. 8). The Spirit's unutterable groanings in our hearts are understood by the Father who listens for the cry of his helpless children (Rom. viii. 26 f.).

CHAPTER VI

The Relation of God to His World.

"As thou didst send me into the world, even so sent I them into the world" (John xvii. 18).

WE have no formal discussion of cosmological theories by Jesus nor does he use technical phrases about this theme. In this as in all things Jesus uses the language of life and not the systematized expressions of the schools.

The World View of Jesus

It need not, however, be assumed that Jesus did not have a world view, a *welt-*

anschauung. Jesus had a world view, but used the term in a variety of senses. He felt himself apart from "this world" and came "for judgment" into it (John ix. 39). I am come a light into the world" (John xii. 46). He even said: "I am the light of the world" (John viii. 12). His primary object in coming is not simply to judge, "but to save the world" (John xii. 47). Clearly then Jesus had a world outlook. He took the world upon his heart in a large way and did not have a limited world range. Satan offered him in subtle temptation "all the kingdoms of the world and the glory of them" (Matt. iv. 8), the goal of Alexander's ambition, of the Cæsars, of Napoleon. We may not, then, dismiss what Christ has to say on this subject with the idea that Jesus was merely a narrow provincial of Judea who had no world ideas of importance.

We must remember that his favorite title for himself was "The Son of man," by which he meant not merely a man, but the representative man, the son of the race who gathered up in himself the ideals and hopes of the best in the world, the man who was such as God meant him to be. As Son of man and Son of God Jesus had the largest and the truest outlook on the world of any man who has ever lived. He can tell us what God the Father thinks of the world and how men should regard it. "The things which I heard from him, these speak I unto the world" (John viii. 27). The words of John reinforce, if need be, this claim of Jesus, for "all things were made by him; and without him was not anything made" (John i. 3). "He was in the world, and the world was made by him, and the world knew him not" (John i. 10). It is presumptuous, then, to say the least, to posit ignorance of the world by Christ, the Creator of the world. How much in his human state Jesus condescended not to know, or did not know, since he grew in knowledge, we do not understand. But certainly we cannot limit his knowledge of the world as that of a mere man of the first century in Judea.

The Senses in Which the Term World is Used by Jesus

It is in the Gospel of John that we find the word "world" used so much. In Mark and Luke each it occurs three times only and but nine times in Matthew. In John we have it 78 times and only 184 in all the rest of the New Testament. How is it used? The usual word for world as used by Jesus is *cosmos.* Twice only does he use the word *oikoumene,* the inhabited earth, and both of these are in the discourse on the Mount of Olives concerning the destruction of Jerusalem and the Second Coming (Matt. xxiv. 14; Luke xxi. 26). Here the world is the earth as the habitation of men. *Cosmos* meant originally orderly arrangement, then ornament as in 1 Pet. iii. 3, "the outward adorning of braiding the hair." It was natural for this word to be applied to the orderly and ornamental arrangement of the universe. So Jesus speaks of the glory which he had with the Father "before the world was" (John xvii. 5), where he uses it for the universe itself. The word is also used by Jesus for the earth simply when he says: "If a man walk in the day, he stumbleth not, because he seeth the light of this world" (John xi. 9), again: "I am no more in the world" (John xvii. 11). Then also we find the Master using the term for the inhabitants of the earth, as when he said: "I came out from the Father, and am come into the world" (John xvi. 28). So also: "The field is the world" (Matt. xiii. 38).

Besides Jesus spoke of the world as sinful and different from his disciples: "If ye were of the world, the world would love its own, but because ye are not of the world, but I chose you out of the world, therefore the world hateth you" (John xv. 19). Again Christ conceived of this world as distinct from the world to come: "Ye are from beneath; I am from above; ye are of this world; I am not of this world" (John viii. 23). Thus he spoke to his enemies after the feast of tabernacles. To Pontius Pilate Jesus said simply: "My kingdom is not of this world" (John xviii. 36). Clearly then the term had a varied content in the mind of Christ. He had a world consciousness and knew that he had entered upon a world conflict and was to win a world conquest.

God the Author of the Universe

With Jesus the world had a "beginning" (Matt. xxiv. 21) and so is not eternal. He will say at the judgment: "Come ye blessed of my Father, inherit the kingdom prepared for you from the foundation of the world" (Matt. xxv. 34).

There was a time when he had glory "before the world was" (John xvii. 5). Moreover, the world will have an end (Matt. xxviii. 20), though here another word (*aion*) is used which means age. Jesus speaks of Satan as the prince of this world, but he will be cast out (John xii. 31). He by no means acknowledges Satan as the creator or rightful master of the world. He is distinctly a usurper who will be displaced by Christ. Jesus does not in so many words say that God created the universe, but that is the whole implication of what he does say in the passages already quoted. His idea is evidently the same as that of John who speaks of the world as being created by the Logos (Christ) who is the Son of God (John i. 10). The Father is the ultimate creator and the Son wrought the Father's will. Jesus called himself "the light of the world" (John vii. 12), but was doubtless here speaking of moral and spiritual light, though he is in fact the force that holds the universe together as Paul shows (Col. i. 17). He is indeed the life of the world (John vi. 33; xi. 25) in every sense of that term. It is not possible to reconcile the teaching of Jesus about the Father's relation to the world with materialism in any form. Naturalistic evolution is repugnant to the fundamental conceptions of Jesus. So is every theory that postulates the eternity of matter.

Hence God is More than the Universe

The immanence of God as Father and as Son is implicit in many of the sayings of Jesus. There is no divorce between God and his world. When Jesus calls himself the light and the life of the world, he is doubtless thinking of the moral and spiritual life of men. This is the main thing. God himself is spirit and our immortal souls are our main concern. "For what doth it profit a man, to gain the whole world, and forfeit his life?" (Mark viii. 36). But Jesus spoke also to the winds and the waves and they obeyed his will (Mark iv. 41). Jesus does not think it incongruous for the divine will to be exercised on inanimate nature. The loaves and fishes alike respond to his call and thus testify to the immanent power of God (Mark vi. 41).

But if God is present in his world, he is more than his world. The world is not God in any sense of the term, whether the universe, the earth, the people, or moral evil in the world. This last certainly was other than God and is due to the devil who is under sufferance in the world and whose dark mysterious existence and power over men Jesus does not explain, though he freely recognizes his baleful influence. But when Jesus says God is spirit (John iv. 24) he pointedly denies that the material universe is God or a part of God, thus rejecting pantheism and monism. What is true of the whole is true of the parts, and so neither the earth nor humanity can be God. God is a Spirit and a Person who has supreme power over the universe. It is his world for he made it. It is the expression of his will, but there is a difference between subject and object. The creative activity of the Father is continuous. He has not tied himself up in his own laws, but exerts a constant control in nature. "My Father worketh even until now, and I work" (John v. 17).

God has life in himself and has given the Son to have life in himself (John v. 26). Spontaneous generation is a futile theory, for life is in God. It is not strange then that the greatest modern scientists, even those who are not Christians or even theists as Spencer and Huxley, frankly confess their ignorance of the mystery of life. Life cannot be put under the microscope. It is not a chemical process nor a part of a cell tissue. Life is in God. God alone gives life as he wills. Life works the cells and builds the marvellous structures in the physical world. But life will never be shown to be a mere mechanical process. Not even radium is life as some excited materialists are saying. God is life.

God Loves the World

God does not acknowledge the devil's claim to ownership of the world. There is evil, terrible evil in the world. It was a good world when God made it. It is a marred and ruined world now, but none the less God loves it. His pity towards it is all the greater because of the evil wrought in it. God does not view with unconcern the moral situation in the world. If Jesus did not himself speak the words recorded in John iii. 16, as possibly he did not, they at any rate fully express his revelation of the Father's attitude toward the world: "For God so loved the world, that he gave his only begotten Son, that whosoever believeth on him should not perish, but have eternal life." God does not wish the world to perish, nor any part of it. "For God," the passage (John iii. 17) continues, "sent not the Son into the world to condemn the world; but that the world should be saved through him."

The Father has indeed "given all judgment unto the Son" (John v. 22), but the Father prefers that in every case the Son shall bring salvation rather than condemnation. "For I came not to judge the world, but to save the world" (John xii. 47). "To save the world." That is the profoundest philosophy of Christianity as expounded by the author of the gospel. The Father wished to bring back to himself a world that had wandered away from him. This is the tragedy of the universe. This is the story of divine love that dwarfs into littleness all others. The Father gave his only begotten son for a world that had learned to hate its Creator, that had spurned a Father's love, and that refused to come back home and be reconciled. To bring harmony into the universe again, to save the lost, the Son gave his own life a ransom on the cross, a victim to the hate of the world for which he died. This cruel death was necessary as a basis for the atoning work of the Son and to make it possible for the Father to save those that believe. But it is none the less the climax of human sin.

The attitude of the Father towards publicans and sinners on the one hand and the self-righteous Scribes and Pharisees on the other is set forth in a matchless manner in the great parable of the Prodigal Son (Luke xv. 11-32). We shall need to come back to this parable again under another point of view. But here let us see the Father's desire that both the elder and the younger sons should dwell in his house. He did not drive the younger away nor did he make him come back, but, O, what a welcome he gave him when he did come back with a repentant heart. He did not make the elder brother sulk in the fields, but he would not drive away the lost son now found again, not even to please the elder brother. The heart of God yearns for the world to be his. For this purpose Christ sent the disciples on their world-wide mission (Matt. xxviii. 19). The conquest of the world, no more no less, is the goal of Christianity, the furthest reach of the Father's love.

But His Kingdom is not of This World

If it were, there would be no need of it and no room for it. If Christianity is "other-worldliness," that is precisely the thing most needed for the world. The world's hunger is for something other than itself, something to make it better than it is. No world-originated system could or can make the world better than the world. Hell was tugging at the world to pull it down and was already victor. The only hope was from above. The constant claim of Jesus was: "I am from above" (John viii. 23). The kingdom that he set up was not of this world (John xviii. 36), was prepared for them before the foundation of the world (Matt. xxv. 34), was an invisible kingdom in the heart (Luke xvii. 20 f.), and was to win. "I have overcome the world" (John xvi. 33), Jesus said. He spoke as a Conqueror and he is still conquering. "In the world ye have tribulation; but be of good cheer" (John xvi. 33). The day will come when "the kingdom of the world is become the kingdom of our Lord and of his Christ" (Rev. xi. 15). Till then God is in Christ reconciling the world to himself. We are the messengers of God and Christ to speed the message, to further the mission of Christ to the world, to win the world to Christ, for he alone can bless and save a world lost in sin.

CHAPTER VII

Relation of God to the Unsaved.

" For the Son of man came to seek and to save that which was lost" (Luke xix. 10).

ARE the wicked children of God? That depends upon what one means by the term "children of God." Is God the Father of the unsaved? That likewise depends on the idea in the term "Father." As in most controversies, the terms need definition if we are to proceed intelligently in the apprehension of the relation of God to the unsaved. The expression "universal fatherhood of God" has become a party shibboleth to some extent in our day. Not always do the persons who use it understand each other. The Universalists mean that all men are indeed the spiritual children of God and will be members of the family of God in heaven. Those who hold the other extreme deny that any are in any sense the children of God save those who are born again into the family of God by the renewal of heart through the Holy Spirit.

We were Created in the Image of God

This early statement in Genesis is accepted by all as an accurate statement of man's original spiritual condition except it be anti-Christian evolutionists who deny the spiritual kinship to God. The original likeness to God is in the spirit, not in the body which is of the earth. But on the physical side we are the children of God in the sense that he is the Creator of all things. But clearly more than this is involved in the image of God which was stamped in our souls. God has relations to men that he does not have to the beasts of the field.

Alienation from God

The background of the life and work of Christ is just this. The world had gone away from God. The world was lost. Something had come in to break the previous relation to God. No longer are men, save an elect few, on terms of fellowship with God. They are outcasts from the family of God, aliens from the commonwealth of Israel, without God, in fact hostile towards God. If such men are still children of God, they are disobedient children who have rebelled against the Father, who have left home, and who have gone over to the enemy of the Father. They have caused themselves to be disinherited, have sold their birthright, and have refused all overtures to return to the Father's love and home. This in fact seems to be the conception of the unsaved that underlies the teaching of Jesus. Hence it is that not all who hear the glad news of salvation will be saved. They are in the enemy's country and will not give up their new pleasures for what they have left and may get by returning. When the seed is sown, the soil may be very hard and beaten, or stony, or thorny. Or perhaps the tares grow right in the midst of the wheat. "The good seed, then, are the sons of the kingdom; and the tares the sons of the evil one" (Matt. xiii. 38 f.). Here "good" is not good by nature, but by virtue of the choice to become sons of the kingdom.

The Condemnation of the Father

The unsaved are under the displeasure of the Father. If John the Baptist called the Pharisees "offspring of vipers" (Matt. iii. 7), so did Jesus: "Ye offspring of vipers, how can ye, being evil, speak good things?" (Matt. xii. 34). This was at the time of the blasphemous accusation. But at the close of the terrible denunciation on the last day in the temple, when Christ let loose the pent up indignation of the years, he said: "Ye serpents, ye offspring of vipers, how shall ye escape the judgment of hell?" (Matt. xxiii. 33). He had poured vials of wrath against these consummate hypocrites who juggled with the consciences of men and the teachings of God and made their proselytes twofold more sons of hell than they were themselves (Matt. xxii. 15).

Certainly there was unusual provocation to have called forth such denunciation from the gentle Christ who was a volcano only to the enemies of God his Father. And yet the fact that Jesus could with justice so characterize these men makes it impossible to think of them as actually belonging to the family of God. They can only be called renegade children. They had accused Jesus of being in league with Satan and thus having power to cast out demons, when in fact they were themselves guilty of the unpardonable sin in thus attributing the manifest work of the Holy Spirit to the devil (Matt. xii. 31 f.). They are "guilty of an eternal sin" (Mark iii. 29). Again in a strenuous controversy with the Pharisees in Jerusalem at the feast of tabernacles six months before his death, Jesus expressly denied that they were the children of God, and said in plain terms that they were children of the devil. "If God were your Father, ye would love me" (John viii. 42). "Ye are of your father, the devil, and the lusts of your father it is your will to do" (John viii. 44). They were the literal descendants of Abraham, but were not the spiritual children of Abraham (John viii. 39). So then God had created them; but they now belonged to the family of the devil.

Judas is repeatedly said to belong to the devil (as John vi. 70). The poor demoniacs were wholly under the power of demons, the agents of Satan. It is not possible to deny successfully the reality of the demoniacal possessions and maintain the spiritual supremacy of Christ. The efforts to do so are all futile.

But, it may be replied, these are exceptional cases. They are specimens of the worst elements in society from the spiritual point of view. It yet remains to show that the bulk of the unsaved are not in the family of God. Jesus had pointedly said in the Sermon on the Mount that, unless the righteousness of the people exceeded that of the Scribes and Pharisees they should not enter the kingdom of heaven (Matt. v. 20). Later he accused the Pharisees of making void the word of God because of their tradition (Matt. xv. 6). But Jesus made a much broader statement when he said to the Galilean throng in the synagogue at Capernaum: "No man can come to me except the Father which sent me draw him" (John vi. 44). This he said when he was explaining to the unspiritual populace that he was a spiritual Messiah. This announcement helped to break the charm of his power over them. If that was the kind of Messiah that he claimed to be, and not a great Jewish king, they wished none of him. But the whole passage serves to show the distance from God and Christ at which the unspiritual multitude dwells. It is not merely the leaders who are away from the Father, but the people as well. "Ye have seen me, and yet believe not" (John vi. 36). More than all this, the impulse to come to Christ comes from the Father. It is a hopeless situation out of Christ, what Paul calls "dead in trespasses and sins." Christ even speaks of "this evil generation" (Matt. xii. 45). Christ is himself the test of character and the door to eternal life. "No one cometh unto the Father, but by me" (John xiv. 6). All who do not thus "come" by him are lost. "He that believeth not has been judged already" (John iii. 18). If this last passage is the teaching of the evangelist only, it is certainly in harmony with the teaching of Jesus as to the condition of the unsaved.

Hell and Eternal Punishment

Jesus taught that the wicked would spend eternity in hell in the outer darkness away from the presence of the Father. "The outer darkness" (Matt. viii. 12; xxii. 13; xxv. 30) is one of the most vivid descriptions of the state of the lost used by the Master. They are away from God who is light, away from the company of the redeemed. Another picture is presented under the image of the undying worm: "where their worm dieth not" (Mark ix. 48). Hades does not mean place of torment itself, but merely the unseen world; yet in Luke xvi. 23 it is used evidently for that part of the unseen world where torment is, for the wicked rich man in Hades "lifted up his eyes, being in torments." This is not a temporary state for "there is a great gulf fixed" (Luke xvi. 26) between the wicked rich man and Lazarus. This is a parable, but it correctly represents Christ's idea of the fate of the wicked. Moreover, Jesus often expressly uses the term Gehenna for the place of the lost. It is not simply "the hell of fire" (Matt. v. 22), but the place where the soul and body of the wicked are sent by God the Father (Matt. x. 28). It is impossible for the Pharisees whom Jesus denounced to escape Gehenna (Matt. xxiii. 33). These are terrible pictures of a place and state of eternal punishment. Certainly they do not have to be taken literally any more than the picture of heaven as a city with streets and river. But the figure in both cases falls short of the reality. Each man makes a hell for himself in the memory of his sin and the lashing of his conscience. The law of heredity reinforces the teaching about hell. If there is eternal progress in holiness, there is also eternal progress in evil. We must not let sentimental notions about the fatherhood of God destroy the real teaching of Christ about the Father. Jesus himself called the wicked "lost" (Luke xix. 10). At the judgment day he will say: "Depart from me, ye cursed, into the eternal fire which is prepared for the devil and his angels" (Matt. xxv. 41). This awful doom is solemnly repeated in measured words at the close of the same discourse on the Mount of Olives: "And these shall go away into eternal punishment: but the righteous into eternal life" (Matt. xxv. 46). It is useless to seek to whittle away the meaning of "eternal" with "punishment." It is the very word that is used with "life." The arguments that will disprove the eternity of the "fire" and the "punishment" will likewise destroy the eternity of the "life." They stand or fall together. Hence we are not to say that God is the Father of all men in the sense that he will not punish unforgiven sin. To say that is not only to contradict the plain teaching of Christ on the subject, but is also to have an inadequate conception of sin, God's view of sin, and God's own nature.

God Seeking his Lost Children

But least of all should we attribute malice to the Father in the punishment of the unsaved. Jesus not only taught us to pray for our enemies, but he did so himself as he hung on the cross (according to what is probably the correct text in Luke xxiii. 34): "Father, forgive them; for they know not what they do." The three immortal parables in the fifteenth chapter of Luke show us the yearning love of the Father for the lost. If the shepherd goes after the one lost sheep, so the Father has sent his Son to save the publicans and sinners. And there is joy in heaven when the lost is found. If the woman searches for the lost piece of money and rejoices when she finds it, so there is joy in the presence of the angels of God over one sinner that repenteth. But this is not all. If the prodigal son, after wandering in sin, repents and comes back with humble confession on his lips, he finds the Father watching for him. "For this my son was dead, and is alive again; he was lost, and is found" (Luke xv. 24). That is it. The lost children are dead children, dead to the influence of the Father's love, and have lost connection with him. This is precisely the work of Christ, to bring to life again the dead children, to find the lost sons and daughters, and bring them home again (John v. 25).

Reconciliation Possible in Christ

But there must first be reconciliation. Home will not be home so long as the wicked feel as they do toward the Father. Christ's blood "is shed for many unto remission of sins" (Matt. xxvi. 28). He gave his "life a ransom for many" (Mark x. 45). This was not an accident. The death of the Son was part of the plan of the Father, who "gave his only begotten Son, that whosoever believeth on him should not perish, but have eternal life" (John iii. 16). The death of Christ was known to him from the beginning of his ministry. He knew that they would destroy the temple of his body and that he would raise it again (John ii. 19). He was the bridegroom who would be taken away (Mark ii. 20). He died not as an example to men, but to save men. His death for sin forms the basis of the reconciling grace of God. God provided the sacrifice for sin in the voluntary offering of his Son. This basis for reconciliation makes it possible for the love of God which sent the Son to offer pardon for sin. But the pardon must be accepted. There must be confession of sin. The prodigal son cannot come back with a rebellious heart as if he had never been away. He would not be happy if he did so come. To confess a wrong is the only manly thing to do. The culprit cannot make atonement, but he can make confession. God himself has provided the atonement in Christ, but the sinner must confess his guilt. This is the straightforward plan of redemption as taught by Jesus. Thus the Father will win back the erring children who have gone astray, who have lost their place in the Father's family, and who are willing to come back on the Father's terms. They are gracious terms and bear hard on none.

Surely the Father could ask no less than loving obedience when he offers so much. He has already shown his own boundless love for sinners in the gift of his Son. He has a right to expect love and service in return. To those who will love Christ, the door is opened wide. "But as many as received him, to them gave he the right to become children of God, even to them that believe on his name" (John i. 12). This is John's interpretation of the relation between God and the unsaved. Christ offers the "right" of sonship to every one who will believe on his name. This is the only way for those who have lost their spiritual birthright (and all have) to get it back. We must "become children of God."

Otherwise the Condemnation Remains

God is love. This is the greatest fact about God. God is the Father. Jesus made this plainer to men than it ever was before. But these great and glorious truths do not exhaust the truth about God. He is the "Holy Father" (John xvii. 11) and the "Righteous Father" (John xvii. 25). This righteousness is as true as his fatherly love, in fact his love is shown in his fatherly righteousness. He is absolutely "good" and alone in such goodness (Mark x. 18). He will not pass transgression by without satisfaction to his own sense of right. For sin is with God a terrible reality, not a mere accident, misfortune, or disease. He holds us responsible for our sins. We are guilty. God is willing to accept, in fact himself provided, the priestly sacrifice of his own Son for human sin. That is the limit of even divine love. The depth of the riches of the love of God in Christ no man will ever know. To refuse such love confirms eternally the condemnation already resting on the sinner who deserves his punishment, who has sinned against the light of nature, conscience, and often even revelation. The awful cloud of the wrath of the Father rests on the rebellious children who have spurned his love and mercy. No wrath is quite so terrible as the righteous wrath of a loving Father. A chief punishment in that wrath will be eternal banishment from the Father's face.

CHAPTER VIII

Relation of God to Believers.

"If a man love me, he will keep my word: and my Father will love him, and we will come unto him, and make our abode with him" (John xiv. 23).

Is God the Father of all Men

CLEARLY it is not true that unregenerate men are no more the children of God than the beasts of the field. It is true that some scientists conceive that all animals have souls, that in the spiritual realm men differ from other animals only in degree, not in nature. But, whether in degree or nature, men are like God in a sense not true of the lower animals. Man is indeed the crown of God's creation and his destiny puts him far above other created beings in the world. But, while all this is true, the general Fatherhood of God, which has an element of truth in it, and a very precious truth, has been much overworked in our day. It is by no means the case that men have only to recognize the fact that they are the children of God in order to enter into the privileges of sonship. The sin of which men are guilty towards God cannot be covered up in such a cavalier fashion as that.

If in one sense men are naturally children of God, in another they are by nature children of wrath, being born in sin and conceived in iniquity. Besides inheriting original sin they become such disobedient children that they have forfeited all claims to the Father's favor, have left his love and care, gone to the enemy's country, and can be called the children of the world, in fact the children of the devil. This is the actual situation which must not be obscured by the truth that is contained in the general fatherhood of God over men, a fatherhood made inoperative by sin. The rebellious child, poisoned by sin, has been justly disinherited by the Father. He can no longer call God his Father.

Becoming Sons of God

So serious and vital is the restoration to the favor of God that it is spoken of by Jesus as a new birth. "Except a man be born anew, he cannot see the kingdom of God (John iii. 3). Nicodemus stumbled helplessly before this radical truth. Three times Christ earnestly and solemnly reiterated that we must be born anew or from above, if we are to enter the kingdom of God. In the spiritual life, then, we must start all over again as a little child begins his life. The entrance upon the new life is a birth of the Spirit of God (John iii. 5, 7). So far have we fallen from our high spiritual estate that we are lost. We have broken connection with God, and are utterly unable to restore it. Until we obtain this initial spiritual experience signified by the new birth, we cannot lay claim to membership in the kingdom of God. By this new birth we at once enter upon the privileges and blessings of the kingdom. It is not possible to make this language of Jesus signify merely a recognition of sonship on man's part. It is a vital religious experience by which one enters into definite relation with God.

It is true that this is a restoration of a relation that once existed between God and man in the beginning, a relation that was broken by man's sin. To all intents and purposes it is a new relation. We must begin *de novo* and can claim no "rights" by reason of the beginning. God's love has brooded over us in all the ages, has planned the means by which we may return to his favor, but none the less he demands a definite experience, the obtaining a new heart on the part of the one who comes back to him. There must be a positive turning away from sin and a definite acceptance of God as Father and Christ as Saviour from sin. The New Testament calls this experience on man's side repentance, conversion, and faith. But this great surrender to God is due in every case to the work of the Holy Spirit and is in connection with, and logically the result of, the new birth of the Spirit. The Father enables those who believe to become his children. "But as many as received him, to them gave he the right to become children of God, even to them that believe on his name" (John i. 12). It is the Evangelist who says this and he is speaking of the Son. It is only through the Son that the Father opens the door to his love. The "right" or "power," it will be observed, is a *gift*. We cannot claim any "rights" with God save justice. That we shall receive, and that is our very undoing, for eternal punishment is retributive and not corrective. This life is the probation period. The future life is the place of eternal states with rewards and restrictions. The "right" to "become" children of God will be "given" to them that believe.

Here we face one of the ultimate problems in theology, the relation between divine sovereignty and human free agency. We know both to be facts, but we are unable to offer any solution of the relation between them. We may be sure that the exercise of God's elective grace is in love, that it respects man's independence, and that it gives no one a ground of complaint against God. We may also freely preach a universal gospel which is the power of God unto salvation to all who believe. God does not appoint the ministers of the Word to select the subjects of his grace. He does that himself. Ours to offer a free gospel to all and press it home on the hearts of men. God will be faithful to his part of the work. Hyper-Calvinism is as unscriptural as extreme Arminianism. Neither point of view embraces the whole truth. We must "believe on his name," but we are "born, not of blood, nor of the will of the flesh, nor of the will of man, but of God" (John i. 13). This is what Paul calls "adoption" (Rom. viii. 15), "whereby we cry, Abba, Father." The signal and the supreme truth in it all is that the Father has made it possible for us to become his children in the real and vital sense.

The Choice of the Father and the Choice of the Child

No one can come unto Christ unless the Father draw him (John vi. 44). God is life and the sinner is dead. His will is ruined by sin. He loves sin and is at home with selfish gratification and indulgence. The impulse to return to God must come from God. Out of the mass of rebellious sinners, who are no longer in his family, the Father chooses the elect, those whom he wills to be his. It is idle for us to speculate about the grounds of this choice. There is no merit in any of us. We have all sinned and come short. Nor do we know the processes by which the Spirit of God works. But we know this. The rebellious child must will to come back. His own will must respond to the will of the Father. In the blending of the will of the Father and the will of the repentant sinner we have the great initial experience of the Christian life. The will is king in the realm of spirit. It is a solemn crisis when the awakened conscience battles for the spiritual victory. "Ye will not come to me, that ye may have life" (John v. 40). It is just this element of will, of choice, that gives moral character to the acts of men, that makes us godlike in prerogative.

Reconciliation is the favorite term of Paul for this spiritual process. It is not used by Jesus, but the idea occurs at every turn. The Father was looking for the prodigal to return and was glad to hear the words of confession from his lips. The joy in the heart of the Father and of the new-found son is the joy of reconciliation. Likewise there is "joy in heaven over one sinner that repenteth" (Luke xv. 7) as is brought out in the story of the lost sheep and also of the lost coin (Luke xv. 10), though, to be sure, the element of reconciliation is not distinctly emphasized. "Forgive" is a word that Jesus often uses of the Father in relation to the sinner (Matt. vi. 14 f.). God does not forgive our sins without reparation. The outraged law must be satisfied. Jesus therefore offered himself a "ransom for many" (Matt. xx. 28). The death of Christ makes a basis for reconciliation. The cross is the hardest word that can be spoken against sin. It cost the Father the blood of his own Son to make it possible to forgive sinners. But the basis of reconciliation is not actual reconciliation. The work is not fully achieved till the sinner accepts heartily the terms of reconciliation. Then he comes to God and is restored to the family of God. The choice to become a child of God is the highest exercise of man's moral nature. If the Father chooses the child and adopts him into his blessed family, no less the child chooses the Father and wills to become a member of this glorious household of faith.

How does the Father feel towards those wayward children who have wandered astray? If we knew the terrible heinousness of sin and the bright holiness of God, we might answer. The nearest parallel that we can find is in the lives of boys and girls who have brought disgrace on the family name. They are outcasts. Their names are never mentioned. Indignation, just indignation, is felt by father and mother, at the treatment such children have given them. And yet, along with the indignation, there is unutterable sorrow and deathless yearning for the lost son, the lost daughter. Detectives may be employed to find them. Message after message may be sent that forgiveness awaits them if they will repent and come back. There is the trouble, that word "repent." In desperation one day the son or daughter comes back with a broken heart and confesses all. This is a poor parallel and fails at many points, most of all in the failure to set forth the awfulness of sin and the need of propitiation, not mere confession. But the double emotion of righteous anger and compassionate love is set forth. Let us in all our theories and explanations never wander from the circle of God's surpassing love, a love that held not back the Son himself that some of the lost might be found, a love too holy to forgive without justice to his own sense of right and confession by the sinner.

The Privileges of Children of God

The first one is the right to say "Father" again. That of itself is worth more than all that the kingdom of Satan offers. The first word that the prodigal was going to say and did say on his return was "Father." He did not wish to say it in his sinful exile. We need not, nor perhaps can we, decide in each instance when Jesus says "Your Father" whether the audience was composed wholly of disciples or not. Certainly in the Sermon on the Mount, when he uses "Father" in relation to men sixteen times, he was addressing the disciples in the presence of a mixed multitude according to both Matthew and Luke. The same thing is true in Matt. xiii. But if he does so speak, this fact would not mean, when he says "Your Father" that he was contemplating under this expression those who were rebellious children and whom he elsewhere calls children of the devil. Let us acknowledge at once that when Jesus says "Thy Father," "our Father," "your Father," "your heavenly Father," he has in mind those who are in vital relation with the Father, the members of the family of God, the kingdom of heaven. Jesus does not say that the unsaved are already children of God. But this fact by no means proves that the unsaved are not disinherited children, lost children of God, whom the Father is anxious to save, and whom the Son came to save. Who are the saved in truth but the lost children who have been found? Before they were found they were just like the rest not yet found. The once lost but now found child can say "Father." That is his privilege.

Prayer is the breath, the atmosphere of the children of God. Gratitude and petition are on the lips of the child and in his heart as he communes with his Father. The coldly critical spirit that looks on prayer as an "interference" with the laws of God has a pitifully narrow idea of the life between father and child. Jesus taught the disciples to pray and say "Our Father" (Matt. vi. 9). It is idle to ask if the unsaved can pray. Certainly they can, but it is not communion of spirit such as the restored child enjoys. It is rather a cry in the dark, a cry for help, for mercy. Such a cry is heard, but the richness of prayer belongs to the soul that has come back to the Father and rejoices in his love.

There is fear still in the child's heart towards the Father. It is sad to see a child lose fear for his father, for he has lost respect for him. The Christian has small ground to fear those who can harm only the body, but we all should fear God (Matt. x. 28–30), both in the sense of reverence and dread, though finally perfect love casteth out fear. Our love for God must not be flippant, effervescent, nor too familiar. The sense of fear is necessary to the high and holy love which should burn in our hearts towards the Lord of All. Such fear will not prevent the blessed peace and fellowship which constitute the kingdom of heaven as an inner state of the heart. This fellowship rests on trust, and trust is just the essential bond between us and God. He demands our confidence. He has done enough for us to deserve our unhesitating trust for present and future. He has a full hand of spiritual mercies for the child who exercises unreserved trust. This is the privilege of a child of God, to trust him. "Be not anxious" is the message that Jesus brings as the secret of a happy life. Put your treasure in heaven, "for where your treasure is, there will your heart be also" (Luke xii. 34).

The Father's Care

Such trust is amply justified on the part of God's children. Why worry about food and raiment? "Your heavenly Father knoweth that ye have need of all these things" (Matt. vi. 32). Look at the lilies of the field in their royal purple. See the birds of the heaven as they carol their joy. Look at the sparrows, not one of whom is forgotten in the sight of God. "But the very hairs of your head are all numbered. Fear not; ye are of more value than many sparrows" (Luke xii. 6 f.) These and other strong expressions Jesus used to set forth the providential care of the Father for his children.

The teaching lifts man into dignity. If God cares this much for men, they must be worth something. Clearly Jesus put a higher estimate upon a man than those who make him merely the victim of iron laws, mechanical forces. The supreme truth here is that God does have a special care for his children, for those who trust him. It is the love of the Almighty Father that finds the petty details of human life not too small for his interest and concern. He does the least: he counts the hairs of our head. He does the greatest; he gives us the Holy Spirit. He does everything for us that makes for our spiritual well-being. Not that he abrogates the laws of life nor removes from us the necessity of personal activity and struggle with our environment. But the Father knows, cares, and helps. All else is easy when this is true. The Father and the Son make their abode with the believer (John xiv. 23). The union with Christ secures union with the Father, a union that is vital and eternal and fruitful (John xv. 1–10).

The Duties of Children

Willing obedience is the highest form that love can take towards one's father.

It should not be a cross to hearken to the voice of God, if we really love him. The reason that children find it hard to obey is because self is assertive. But in the religious life the very essence of spirituality is submission to the will of God. It is sin that makes the child set himself in resistance to the father. Obedience does not save, but obedience is a test of salvation. By their fruits ye shall know them. By obedience we find the doors opened to spiritual growth. If any man is willing to do his will, he shall know of the teaching. It is not enough for the child of God to talk about the privileges of sonship and disregard God's purpose. We are saved to serve.

Jesus sends us forth as the Father sent him. We cannot call ourselves loyal sons of God because we have correct ideas of the way men become children of God while we lead disobedient and sinful lives. We must hear the call of God to send the gospel to all the world as well as to have correct teaching and lead holy lives. As with Christ, so with us, our meat and drink should be to do the will of our Father. If the Father and the Son really dwell in us, this will be our highest joy. Duty becomes happiness, for our self-will is lost in the will of our Father whose we are and whom we serve. "If ye love me, ye will keep my commandments" (John xiv. 15).

The Destiny of Children

It is to be with the Father forever. For this purpose the Son will come again and take us to the Father. He has "many mansions" ready. He comes, we may believe, in the death of every believer and takes him to God. He will come to raise the bodies of all in the end. Meanwhile the child is to be like the Father. He is to be perfect as the Father is perfect (Matt. v. 48). He is to be, for example, merciful as the Father is merciful (Luke vi. 36). We know little as to the details of heaven and hell. But this much is certain, that hell is the fulfilment of the irrevocable choice of evil made here. It is a continuous confirmation of that love of sin and identification with sin. So heaven is fellowship with the Father and increasing likeness to the Father. "We shall be like him, for we shall see him as he is." Jesus is our Elder Brother and we are to be his brethren. God is his Father in a sense not true of us (John xx. 17), and yet he calls us "brethren." We are his "brothers" and "sisters." "For whosoever shall do the will of God, the same is my brother, and sister, and mother" (Mark iii. 34 f.).

It was to bring this to pass that Jesus left his throne on high, became a servant to men, suffered the rebuffs from the religious leaders of the time, endured the shame of the cross, died for our sins, and rose again. He is not ashamed to call us brethren (Heb. ii. 11). This is the high destiny of those who believe in God the Father and Jesus Christ whom he has sent. These are the real children of God, not those who were the literal descendants of Abraham. The real Israel to Jesus, as to Paul, is the spiritual Israel. The true family of God are the elect who love him, the church for which Jesus died and which he washed with his blood. "Come, ye blessed of my Father, inherit the kingdom prepared for you from the foundation of the world" (Matt. xxv. 34).

CHAPTER IX

Jesus' Conception of God Compared with the Apostolic Teaching.

"He shall glorify me: for he shall take of mine and declare it unto you" (John xvi. 14).

"Being therefore by the right hand of God exalted, and having received of the Father the promise of the Holy Spirit, he hath poured forth this, which ye see and hear" (Acts ii. 33).

"BACK to Christ" has been the watchword of modern New Testament theology. It is a good word to hearken to, provided no unnatural antithesis is made between Jesus and his Apostles. The historical method of Biblical study can be as arbitrary and unreliable in its results as the purely theological method if proper poise and balance be not preserved. It is literally true that it has cost a real struggle for the modern world to brush aside mediæval theological conceptions that obscured the person and teaching of Jesus. The battle for the restoration of the original gospel has been greatly prolonged and is still going on. But the historical Christ stands in clearer outline to-day than at any time since the fourth century A. D.

The Supremacy of Christ

The result is that on all hands men acknowledge the supremacy of Jesus as teacher of religion and morals. His spiritual ideal is the highest that the world has ever had. The moral and spiritual isolation of Jesus is the greatest miracle of the world. The theories of men fail to explain him on grounds of natural development. All do not accept the necessary consequence of his supremacy in character, works, words, and claims. All do not accept him as being the Son of God in essence as well as in character. But still his unique position is unchallenged. Indeed, so sharply does Jesus now stand out against the theological refinements of the middle ages that there is a strong tendency on the part of some to minimize the importance of the Apostolic teaching. The vagaries of the school-men are laid at the door of Paul who is said to have misunderstood Jesus and his teaching and to have rabbinized Christianity. "Less of Paul and more of Christ," they say.

All this has a specious sound and may catch the unthinking. It is a far cry from Paul to Augustine, not to say Anselm or Thomas Aquinas. Is Paul more like Augustine or Jesus in his theology? Undeniably Augustine is much indebted to Paul and may have interpreted Paul at some points apart from his relation to

Jesus; but there is much in Augustine that does not come from Paul or Jesus. It was the boast of Paul that he had a direct revelation of the gospel of Jesus (Gal. i: 11 f.). We take it that mediævalism was a perversion of Paul, not that Paul perverted the teachings of Jesus. At any rate we must not seek for Paul's theology through the eyes of Augustine, but study Paul for ourselves. This is not to say that the world is not under a great debt both to Augustine and Calvin for their interpretations of Paul. But we must not charge Paul with the excesses or excrescences of even the greatest of theological teachers. We have the words of Paul and the words of Jesus.

The First Interpreters of Jesus

This is a happy phrase of a recent writer. We must frankly admit that while the Apostles were with Jesus they failed to understand him. He was not like his environment and they were. They expected a temporal kingdom just before he ascended on the clouds to heaven: "Lord, dost thou at this time restore the kingdom to Israel?" (Acts i. 6). They contended over the first places in such a kingdom even on the night of the betrayal (Luke xxii. 24). Hence also the doubt that held them fast when Jesus rose from the dead. Slowly they were convinced that he had risen from the grave. Along with new faith came new hope and joy, but they were still powerless to carry out the Lord's commission to take the world for him. Nor did they yet apprehend fully either the person of Christ or his teaching. They had indeed a much richer store of material now that Jesus had risen from the grave. They occupied a far better standpoint on this side of the empty tomb. The words of the risen and triumphant Christ were ringing in their ears. But even yet they did not fully grasp the significance of the career of Jesus of Nazareth. But in ten days after Jesus went back to the Father a transformation came over Peter and the rest who were waiting for the promise of the Father (Acts i. 4).

Jesus had promised to send the Holy Spirit to bring all things to their remembrance and to teach them all things (John xiv. 26). "He shall take of mine and declare it unto you" (John xvi. 14). The fulfilment of this promise on the great Day of Pentecost is the cardinal fact in the apostolic history and teaching. These men at once enter upon a distinctly new epoch. They grasp securely and clearly the spiritual significance of the kingdom of God and form a true estimate of the work, person, and teaching of Jesus in connection with it. There will be development after this day, but it will be development in harmony with this epoch. Once Peter will signally fail in courage, not in grasp of spiritual truth (Gal. ii. 11–21), and will woefully sin.

It is not in harmony with the facts to say that after Pentecost the Apostles are as inadequate guides to the teaching of Jesus as they were before. Jesus had said that they would understand all things when the Holy Spirit came, and the record shows the fulfilment of that prophecy.

We cannot then, in view of this teaching of Christ, carelessly brush aside the Apostolic teaching as unnecessary or as incorrect. He expressly said that he had yet many things to say, but that they could not bear them then. "Howbeit when he, the Spirit of truth, is come, he shall guide you into all the truth" (John xvi. 12 f.). Luke begins the Acts by speaking of what "Jesus began both to do and to teach" (Acts i. 1). The Apostolic teaching justifies the prediction of Christ. These first interpreters of Jesus who speak under the new enlightenment of the Holy Spirit strike the same note about the Father that Jesus did. The Acts of the Apostles is a proper sequel to the Gospel of Luke as the author feels and says (Acts i. 1). Peter pointedly identifies the events on the Day of Pentecost as the fulfilment of the promise of the Father which Jesus had made: "This Jesus did God raise up, whereof we are witnesses. Being therefore by the right hand of God exalted, and having received of the Father the promise of the Holy Spirit, he hath poured forth this, which ye see and hear" (Acts ii. 32 f.). Stephen boldly announced the purely spiritual nature of God who "dwelleth not in houses made with hands" (Acts vii. 48), a teaching in exact harmony with that of Jesus to the Samaritan woman (John iv. 21 f.), but entirely too advanced for the ceremonial and sacramental Pharisees who saw in it a desecration of the temple.

It required, it is true, a vision for Peter to see that Gentiles could be saved without first becoming Jews. Jesus had said: "Other sheep I have, which are not of this fold" (John x. 16). Jesus had also made all meats clean when he rebuked the pettifogging Pharisees who had a doctrine about eating with unwashed hands (Mark vii. 19). But it was not till Peter actually stood inside of the house of Cornelius the Gentile that he was able to say: "Of a truth I perceive that God is no respecter of persons: but in every nation he that feareth him, and worketh righteousness, is acceptable to him" (Acts x. 34). He did not mean that Cornelius was already saved before he came, for he expressly states that he was to speak words "whereby thou shalt be saved, thou and all thy house" (Acts xi. 14). What he means is that Cornelius can be saved and remain a Gentile. God will be Father of Gentlies as well as Jews. This is indeed a great light; it is the same light that Jesus shed, but that Peter had until now been too blind to see.

The Gospel Records Later in Date than the Earliest Epistles

The facts just appealed to follow naturally the closing scenes in the Gospels. It may be replied that the Acts of the Apostles was not written till some time after the events here recorded. This is true, but it is also true of the Gospels themselves. In neither case, however, is the testimony properly invalidated. It is evident from the prologue to Luke's Gospel (Luke i. 1-3) that there were written sources before his Gospel was undertaken, probably Mark and Matthew, and still earlier and, perhaps, briefer sketches. There were still also eyewitnesses of the life of Jesus whom Luke consulted. The life and words of Jesus had been preached over a large part of the Roman Empire. Luke was an historian in method and spirit. The same careful accuracy claimed in his Gospel (Luke i. 3) is exhibited in the Acts.

But, while all this is true, it can be justly said to those who seek unduly to depreciate the Apostolic teaching in comparison with that of Jesus that we only have the words of Jesus in the writings of his disciples and followers. If we may not believe the interpretation of John's Epistles, why his Gospel? If Peter's Epistles are to be discredited, why accept Mark's Gospel written under his influence? If Paul is a false interpreter of Jesus, why follow Luke, Paul's companion and admirer? If James, the champion of true Judaism, does not understand Jesus, why listen to Matthew's Jewish Gospel? Certainly I and II Thessalonians antedate the earliest of our Gospels and probably James, I and II Corinthians, Galatians, and Romans, with possibly a number of other Epistles. We must on historical grounds listen to the Apostolic teaching if we wish to preserve the Gospels as genuine records of the teaching of Jesus.

The Earlier and the Later Epistles Give the Same View of the Father

In I Thessalonians, the earliest of Paul's Epistles and dating probably A. D. 52, we find him saying: "God the Father" (i. 1), "our God and Father" (i. 3; iii. 11). Likewise in II Thessalonians, written a few months later, we see him writing, "God our Father" (i. 1; ii. 16). In James we read of "the Father of lights" (i. 17) and of "pure religion and undefiled before our God and Father" (i. 27). So also James says that with the tongue we bless "the Lord and Father" (iii. 9).

In Paul's Epistles of the second and third groups (I and II Cor., Gal. Rom., Phil., Col., Eph.) we meet very often the expressions God the Father, God our Father. The personal letter to Philemon does not so speak of God. In Hebrews xii. 9 God is called "the Father of spirits." In I and II Peter, Jude, I and II John (not III John) we likewise see the expression God the Father. In the Pastoral Epistles God is not specifically called Father, but rather "God our Saviour" (I Tim. i. 1; Titus i. 3; II Tim. i. 10). In the Revelation of John only twice is God called Father (i. 6; xiv. 1) and then he is spoken of as the Father of Jesus the Lamb of God. But there is no radical difference in conception in the various Apostolic writings save in the Pastoral Epistles. This group is dominantly ecclesiastical and soteriological in idea, and hence Paul seems to prefer Saviour to Father. Each writer approaches the idea of God the Father from his own standpoint. But it is the same God and Father of us all who is presented whether in Thessalonians or in Ephesians, whether in James or Paul, whether in John or Peter.

The Teaching of Christ about the Father the Norm of the Apostolic Teaching

The Apostles speak of God as Father much more frequently than do the Old Testament writers. They have caught the new accent of Jesus whose great aim was so to reveal the Father to men that reconciliation would be made between God and man on the basis of his atoning death. The word Father is on the lips of Jesus at every turn and he uses it far more frequently than do the authors of the Acts and Epistles. This is but natural. No one had the right to speak in such familiar terms of the Father as did Jesus. God was his Father in a sense not true of others, and to set forth the Father was his highest aim, while the Apostles, taught by the Spirit, bore witness to Christ. But under the tutelage of the Holy Spirit the teaching of Jesus bears rich results. The Apostles proclaim God as Father in exactly the same sense that Jesus announced him to men.

God is the Father of our Lord Jesus Christ (Eph. i. 3) in a special sense. He is in some sense the Father of all men, as Paul says: "Our God and Father of all, who is over all, and through all, and in all" (Eph. iv. 6), where he seems to be speaking of God in his eternal relations to all the universe, though the context here clearly points to the saved. Compare what Paul said on Mars Hill: "For we are also his offspring. Being thus the offspring of God we ought not to think that the Godhead is like unto gold, or silver, or stone, graven by art and device of man" (Acts xvii. 28 f.).

But this general sonship of all men does not save them. God "commands men that they should all everywhere repent" (Acts xvii. 30). The fact that God is the Father of our spirits does not constitute us members of the family of God, the household of faith. "If any man hath not the spirit of Christ, he is none of his" (Rom. viii. 9). "As many as are led by the Spirit of God, these are sons of God" (Rom. viii. 14). These alone "have the spirit of adoption whereby we cry, Abba, Father." These alone are children of God, heirs of God, and joint heirs with Christ (Rom. viii. 15 f.). This is in exact accord with the teaching of Jesus concerning God the Father who in one sense is the Father of all men, but on the other hand includes in his family and kingdom only those who have been born again, who have made peace with the Father by Christ's death and through a repentant heart. It is probably in this same twofold sense that Paul uses the term Saviour as applied to God when in I Tim. iv. 10 he speaks of God as "the Saviour of all men, specially of them that believe." He sends the rain on all (Acts xiv. 17) as Paul showed at Lystra. But he is Father and Saviour of those that believe in a special and glorious sense not true of those who are still in the "far country" and whose destiny will be the outer darkness away from the Father's home and the Father's love.

CHAPTER X

Jesus' Conception of God the Ruling Idea in Theology.

"Sir, we would see Jesus" (John xii. 21).

"Lord, show us the Father, and it sufficeth us" (John xiv. 8).

IT has been hard for men to see God, though he is not far from any of us. We have blinded our eyes so that we cannot see. We grope helplessly in the dark. The light of reason is clear enough to show us that God is, but sin has such a grip on our wills that we cannot act on this light. We have in our sinful pride wandered away from God. We flounder in a sea of doubt as we struggle back toward God.

Theology a Changing Quantity

There is theology and theology. There is evangelical theology and rationalistic theology. There is sacramental theology and experimental theology. Radical differences divide theology into opposing camps. Some of these lines of divergence reappear in every age. The emphasis on the form as a means of salvation as opposed to the spiritual reality was, if possible, sharper in Christ's day than in ours. Mere traditionalism suits some minds and costs less expenditure of mental energy than a vital spiritual experience. In each type of theology there is growth and adaptation. All life is change, and a live theology is ever seeking new light from the word of life. Theology is man's attempt to interpret the revelation of God in Christ and the Bible and the world. This attempt varies in different men and in different epochs of the world. Each age comes into possession of a new angle of vision, a new vantage ground of interpretation; precisely as science is not absolute, but is ever changing its conceptions of the universe. The truth in the old remains, while the new is tested for its truth.

This is not saying that one form of theology is as good as another. Far from it. The truth is the goal of theology. Much truth has long been won and this cannot be taken away from us. But we do not yet apprehend all truth. We are still pressing on. Theology is not unreliable because of this changing flow of life. It would be unreliable and useless if it were not able to assimilate new truth and adjust itself to new conditions. Life will crack the hardest moulds in rock or mind in time. Theology should be neither old nor new, but embrace the truth in both.

God the Center of all Theology

Theology is the doctrine of God which we formulate. There is this common bond, then, in all theology worthy of the name. It is an honest effort to present orderly conceptions of the truth about God in all his relations, and especially in his relation to man. It is but just to say that while the word theology has God as the center, not all theology preserves this etymological truth. Some theology is man-centered and not God-centered. But clearly the right way to approach the discussion of man is from the point of view of God. We need the man Christ Jesus to show us what God the Father is, but even here he is showing us God, and it is God who has sent his Son in the flesh to reveal himself to us. Christ is not man's effort to find God, but God's endeavor to reveal himself to men. We can never reach the truth about God or man if we put man in the center of our theological system.

Christ the Starting Point of Modern Theology

Christ is the most clearly drawn character in history. His picture fills the eye of the civilized world. It is no mere picture. The reality of this supreme personage is the chief fact in history. His ethical teachings satisfy the demands of the enlightened conscience. His spiritual sympathies touch the hearts of men. He is the world's Ideal become real. Jesus is then the meeting place for those who love God and those who merely love their fellowmen. The theological and the non-theological can find common ground in him. If we expect to win the sceptic, the agnostic, the worldly, the indifferent, the grossly sinful, the only hope of so doing is in Jesus. The modern apologetic, if it is to become effective and not be a mere dialectic, must start with the acknowledged truth in the person of Jesus. The enemies of religion well understand this obstacle in their path. Lines of opposition that start far away from Christ are laid ultimately against his supreme position in the hearts of men. So long as Christ rules the lives of men, Christianity dominates the world.

Christ's Conception of God the Truth

God is absolute and we cannot take in the absolute, for we are finite. Jesus did not reveal God in abstract argument. He revealed God in the concrete, in himself, the only begotten Son. God is like Jesus. If men wish to get definite conceptions of God the Father, let them look at Jesus. Jesus simply, but abruptly said: "I am the truth." We get lost in the mazes of argument and the truth escapes us. In Jesus the truth is transparent and is personified. Hence the revelation of God the Father in Christ is final. The prophecies pointed in outline to him. The Apostles sought by interpretation to explain him. We aim to group together the entire picture in prophecy, historical fact, and interpretation. But we shall fail even thus to see correctly Christ and God in Christ unless we experience God in our hearts. For Christ came not to reveal the Father simply as an intellectual or historical fact, but as a spiritual experience in the life of the sinner. This is ultimate truth verified in the spirit of man who is brought again into vital union with God by the Holy Spirit.

Christ's Conception of God Unifies Revelation

All the slow stages of Israelitish history culminate in the teaching of Jesus about God the Father. The prophets in those different epochs fall into harmony around this great organizing idea. The Apostolic writings flow out normally from this stream of truth. Type finds its fulfilment. Symbol gathers up the love of God in the death of Christ. The spirit conquers the letter. The right interpretation with open Bible and open mind becomes possible. Thus alone the reader gains access to the historical and spiritual interpretation of Scripture.

Christ's Conception of God Satisfies the Reason and the Facts of Life

The reason is not surrendered when one becomes a Christian. Rather is it satisfied. The necessary limitations of the human mind make possible greater freedom in other directions. The first step in intellectual progress is made when one recognizes his limitations. We cannot explain all the problems of the universe. We cannot solve the mysteries in our own complex nature. Jesus himself in his twofold nature is the supreme mystery. And yet, waiving the mystery that is insoluble, the mind has rest in Jesus, the God-man, the mediator between God and man. He satisfies our need of a helper to intercede with God for us. His perfect character commands the allegiance of our hearts. We are willing to listen to such a man when he speaks of the highest and most vital things. The fact of sin calls for a Saviour. Baffled mankind need no longer be beaten by the tempter if refuge be taken in Christ.

To Know God we Must Know Christ

Let this be our last word about Christ and the Father. He would not have come to earth if it had not been necessary. He knew how he would be treated before he came. He offered his life a ransom for many. If men could find God without his help, he would not have come at all. Before the Incarnation, some had found God, it is true. To some God the Father manifested himself directly. To some the Son appeared in a theophany. To some the Holy Spirit spoke. But the world as a whole was in darkness. Even the Jewish world knew not God in spirit and in reality.

When the Son of God came to his own people, descendants of Abraham and natural heirs of the kingdom promised to David, they did not recognize him. His own people knew him not.

But out of the great world Christ has found a spiritual Israel, true sons of God, who have responded to the message which he has brought to men. The Father calls and those who are willing to be his children hear his voice. It is not difficult to find God now, since Jesus has brought him near to our minds, and since the Holy Spirit presses home that message to our hearts. The sublime fellowship of the risen Christ is ours, if we will. "Go unto my brethren, and say to them, I ascend unto my Father and your Father, and my God and your God" (John xx. 17).

The joyful task before the true children of God is to make known Christ's view of the Father. We shall best do this as we help men see Jesus. It is not alone by word of exposition that this sublime work is to be performed. If we walk as Jesus walked, in his spirit and with his ideals, we shall show that God the Father indeed dwells in us.

What the world most hungers for is not intellectual arguments to prove that God exists, but the life that silently, but genuinely witnesses to the presence of God in heart, word, and deed. The practice of the presence of God here and now is the greatest sermon to the unsaved and is the foretaste of heaven itself. If God is to be our Father hereafter, he must be our Father here. Jesus brought God the Father vividly and powerfully to the hearts of men in this life. He left that impression and that reality in the world as a permanent theological conception and as a vital religious experience. The best teacher of the presence and guidance of the Father is he whose life is most like the life of Jesus. The union of the believer with Christ the true Vine should be fruitful. "For to me to live is Christ." That is Paul's motto and no higher can be expected, for that is to let the Incarnate Word rule the life.

CHAPTER XI

Summary.

"I ascend unto my Father and your Father, and my God and your God" (John xx. 17).

IT may be well to take a bird's-eye view of the whole argument as to the Teaching of Jesus concerning God the Father. It is impossible to overestimate the importance of the subject of this volume. It is not exaggeration to say that it is the most vital of all themes to sinful men. The very failure of men to reach adequate truth about God accents the value of the revelation of the Father in the Son. There was much revealed truth about God in the Old Testament, but this was not properly apprehended. It was not till God expressed himself in bodily form in the person of Jesus Christ that the idea of God became real, tangible, sympathetic, winsome, dominating. In Christ the old truth became clearer, and new truth about the Father became possible.

The doctrine of the Trinity becomes thus not only a necessity, but a comforting truth of the Godhead. As Jesus revealed the Father in himself, the Holy Spirit reveals the Son to us that we may know the Father.

God is Lord of creation. He is person and not the material universe. It is God's world, but the world is not God. Men are like God in a sense that animals are not. We bear the image of God in our immortal spirits, an image so blurred by sin that we no longer deserve to be called the children of God who is in fact the Creator of our souls and bodies. But what we have lost can be restored by the new birth of the Holy Spirit. This new spiritual birth is made possible by the atoning death of Christ as the sacrifice for sin. Those who are thus reconciled to God become members of the family of God, enter the kingdom, and have eternal life.

The apostolic teaching is an interpretation of the teaching of Jesus by men who were specially equipped by personal experience with Jesus and his followers. More than this they had also, for Jesus had promised them the Holy Spirit to be their teacher. It is natural and proper that the fundamental and axiomatic truths of Christ should receive fuller expansion in the Apostolic teaching. It is a false antithesis to depreciate the apostolic teaching by the teaching of Jesus. They were not only the first and authoritative interpreters of Christ, but we should not have the words of Jesus save for what they have written. Jesus wrote only in the hearts of men, with the Spirit, not with pen and ink.

The ruling idea in present day theology is Jesus' teaching concerning God the Father. It is bound to be the dominant conception in all spiritual Christianity. A formal theology that hides Christ from men behind theological phrases conceals God from men. It is when men see Christ that they know God. Jesus is the Saviour from sin and not theology, not even orthodox theology. Christo-centric theology is the kind that should enlist the mind and heart of the teacher of men, and even this theology should not come between Christ and the sinful heart.

THE END

INDEX OF SUBJECTS

Q

R

S

T

U

W

Z

INDEX OF TEXTS